GENERATION BY GENERATION

A Modern Approach to the Basics of Genealogy

Drew Smith

Genealogical Publishing Company
Baltimore, Maryland

Published by
Genealogical Publishing Company
Baltimore, Maryland
2023

ISBN 9780806321271

Cover design by Kate Boyer, Heron Creek Press, LLC

Contents

Preface

I'm a lifelong reader, and my very first job in high school was to work in the local public library. I lived in a world of books, especially non-fiction, and over the decades my home bookshelves began to groan under the weight of a huge collection. In 1992, when I first became seriously interested in learning how to research my family's history, I immediately sought out books that would show me how. In those pre-Amazon days (and before the proliferation of mega-bookstores like Borders and Barnes & Noble), this meant my scouring the small bookstores throughout the Tampa Bay area to purchase every genealogy how-to book I could find. Some of these books had been published as far back as the early 1970s, while others had been updated with new editions in the early 1990s. I found these books useful, but for me something still seemed missing in the way they approached research.

Eventually, I became a professional genealogist: not the type who did research for clients, but the type who wrote how-to magazine articles and occasional books about genealogy. I also spoke at local genealogy society meetings, which then led to my speaking at state, national, and international genealogy conferences. I became an administrator for what soon developed into one of the largest genealogy groups on Facebook. I saw my role then and now as a genealogy educator, and I also saw the problems that new genealogists had with getting started.

A few years ago, I began forming my own ideas on how I could write a better beginner's book, a genealogy how-to book that wasn't structured in a traditional way. Traditional beginner books, after discussing home-based sources of information, jumped into describing each type of genealogical record (census, vital records, newspapers, etc.), even when some of those record types weren't immediately relevant to the beginner's needs.

I felt that a genealogy how-to book should be organized in the same way that genealogical research should be done: starting with oneself, then one's living family and relatives, and then moving backwards in time, generation by generation. Each chapter would describe a time period and the kinds of records available for that time period. In that way, one could learn about new types of records just as one needed them.

This is the book you are holding.

This book is the book I wish had existed when I first got serious about genealogy back in 1992. Of course, today there are things like online services (FamilySearch, Ancestry, MyHeritage, Findmypast, etc.) and DNA testing that didn't even exist when I started, but that will make your own first efforts so much more fun and rewarding. I'm a bit envious!

For me, the best part of genealogical writing or speaking is that I learn about things that I didn't know, making me a better genealogical researcher. It also means that I am continually putting myself into the mindset of someone who hasn't done any of this kind of research, someone who needs the process described in plain language. In one very real sense, this book means that you and I are going on a journey together, both of us becoming better at this hobby.

Start your journey with me by reading the Introduction, then the chapters in Part I ("For All Generations - Preparing to Research"). The chapters in Part I will prepare you to better understand the genealogical records that you'll be discovering later. You'll learn about names, places, dates, and events in Chapter 1, relationships among family members in Chapter 2, the genealogical research process itself in Chapter 3, and the tools of software and organizing in Chapter 4. In Chapter 5 you'll be learning how to find what research has already been done on your family, if any. And finally, you'll learn the basics of DNA testing in Chapter 6.

As you move into Part II ("Generation by Generation - Doing the Research"), you'll first learn about using those online websites (Chapter 7). Then we begin the slow and careful journey into the past in the chapters that follow. Chapter 8 starts us in the present and takes us back to 1950. Chapter 9 takes us back to 1880, with a focus on the most useful record types, including those for World Wars I and II. Chapter 10 takes us back to 1850, which covers records for enslaved people and for the U.S. Civil War. Chapter 11 takes us back to 1775, including records for the Revolutionary War and the War of 1812, and when the United States first began to take a decennial census in 1790. Chapter 12 gets us back to the colonial days of British America. Chapter 13 takes us to other countries with significant numbers of records in English (the English-speaking parts of Canada, plus the United Kingdom, Ireland, Australia, and New Zealand). Chapter 14 takes us into countries with records in other languages. And Chapter 15 wraps up the journey.

The most difficult thing about writing any book that discusses technology is how quickly technology changes. While I've made every effort to provide you with the most current screenshots and descriptions of websites available, don't be too surprised if things look a little bit different by the time you yourself visit the same sites. The best thing that a genealogical researcher can do is to be comfortable with change. You'll always be learning something new.

Writing this book wouldn't have been possible without the full support of my publisher, Genealogical Publishing Company (GPC). Joe Garonzik, GPC marketing director, was willing to take a chance on a new beginner's book organized in a non-traditional way. Early chapters were reviewed by GPC editor Marian Hoffman, and after her retirement, GPC editor Denise Larson saw the book to completion. I am grateful for all of their hard work.

Drafts of the early chapters were reviewed with feedback by professional genealogical colleagues Amy E. K. Arner and Paula Stuart-Warren.

I am grateful for the ongoing support I receive from the University of South Florida Libraries. Dean Todd Chavez gets the credit for allowing me to focus so much of my time on supporting the genealogical research of others, whether they be faculty, students, community members, or the general public.

Finally, I was inspired and supported by my husband, George G. Morgan, who published four editions of his own beginner's genealogy book between 2004 and 2015. I had the honor and pleasure of serving as technical editor for each edition.

Lap cat Oxford, who sadly is no longer with us, deserves his own mention.

Introduction

The mysterious lady in my grandmother's parlor

Aunt Annie Mae was a lot of fun. She would visit my Grandmother and Granddaddy Martin on a regular basis in their little green house on Ebenezer Road in my hometown of Newberry, South Carolina. Aunt Annie Mae would sit in the parlor across from Grandmother Martin while sharing the latest family gossip. Even after Granddaddy Martin died in 1964, she continued her visits with Grandmother until Aunt Annie Mae's own death in 1972.

She was clearly family. Yes, I knew of older women in my hometown who everyone called "aunt" even though they weren't related, but I was pretty sure that Aunt Annie Mae wasn't one of those. But how exactly was Aunt Annie Mae related to me? It was a mystery that genealogy could solve. I promise to share the answer with you before the end of this introductory chapter.

As children we learn that every human being is the product of two biological parents, whether or not both individuals are involved in raising their child. (Let me use this opportunity to point out that genealogists are free to research whatever parent or parents they choose, whether biological, step, or adoptive. Don't let anyone tell you differently.)

For our own personal ancestral story, this fact of human origin continues backwards in time, generation by generation. Our story will eventually lead us to people who we don't know, places where we've never visited, and times when things were very different from the way they are now. We might be struck by the fact that if any of these ancestors had made different life choices (who to marry, where to live, what type of work to do, and so on) we wouldn't even exist. Each of their choices plays a part in making us who we are today.

You picked up this book because you have some curiosity about these people, places, and times, but you need help in learning the answers. You may have been born into a family that knows a great deal about its past and shares that information freely. It may turn out that some of what is "known" is wrong, so be prepared to do some research to find out the real story. Or your family may be reluctant to talk about its ancestors. Then again, your family may genuinely know little about its history and may be hoping that you'll be the one to rediscover the information that was forgotten!

So how did I get interested in my own family history?

As I mentioned at the beginning of this introduction, I grew up in Newberry, South Carolina, a town of about 9,000 people when I lived there in the 1960s and early 1970s. Newberry is part of the U.S. Piedmont, that hilly area that exists between the Appalachian Mountains and the flat Atlantic Ocean coastal plain. This reminds me of a joke that is told about cities in the neighboring state of Georgia:

In Atlanta, the first question someone will ask you when they first meet you is "What do you do for a living?", in Macon it's "What church do you go to?", in Augusta it's "Who is your grandmother?", and finally, in Savannah it's "What would you like to drink?" The point of this humorous comparison of Georgia cities is to suggest that the people of Savannah are fun and very welcoming to their guests, without even the need to know anything about their background.

For me, there was some truth about the Augusta part of the joke—no surprise given that Augusta is only 70 miles from Newberry. The same question about my family was asked of me in Newberry by residents who didn't know me. "Who are your people?" I had lots of relatives on my mother's side in Newberry and the surrounding counties, although my mother didn't seem to know much past her own grandparents.

My father's side was from far away in Newark, New Jersey. His brother (Uncle Charlie) and Uncle Charlie's wife and grandson would stop by our South Carolina house every year at Christmas on their way to Fort Lauderdale, Florida, to visit Grandmother Smith. Uncle Charlie did seem to like to talk about their relatives, but my father wasn't quite so much into sharing the stories.

Even if I wanted to know more about my ancestors, I didn't have a clue as to how to go about it. As a kid, I had looked at the genealogy corner in Newberry's public library, but I hadn't found the materials there to be helpful. So, I set aside my interest until January 1992, by which time I was in my mid-30s and living in Tampa, Florida. I was far away from my South Carolina and New Jersey relatives and busy with my career and my own life. Then my favorite aunt, who was my mother's sister Virginia (nicknamed Jenny), died. I returned to Newberry for the funeral. There I saw relatives who I hadn't talked to in years, and it immediately struck me that almost all my parents' siblings were gone. Mom had only one surviving sibling after Aunt Jenny's death, while Dad's only living sibling, Uncle Charlie, died in December of the same year. I felt the pressure of learning about the family while my parents were still alive so that I could share with them what I had learned.

What motivates *you*?

Genealogy is a popular hobby. For some, it's even a profession! But not everyone does it for the same reason. Think about your own motivations, because your motivations may determine how to best go about doing your research.

You may be a fan of history, including the arrival of the Pilgrims in America in 1620. Or the years of the American Revolutionary War in the late 1770s and early 1780s. Or the signing of the Treaty of Guadalupe Hidalgo in 1848, which resulted in Alta California (the modern-day states of California, Nevada, and Utah, plus parts of four other states) becoming part of the United States. You may wonder if you could be descended from the people who were linked in some way to those events. The General Society of *Mayflower* Descendants (the Mayflower Society), the National Society Daughters of the American Revolution (NSDAR), and Los Californianos are examples of three groups, known as lineage societies, that maintain official lists of people directly descended from historical participants. There are numerous lineage societies that celebrate aspects of national, state, or local history. To join a lineage society, you would need to research and document how you are related to the ancestors honored by the society. This means that you would need to focus your research on one specific line of people, from the historical individual down to you. (Note: Lineage societies may require that you are descended *biologically* from the historical ancestor and may not allow adoptees to join through their adoptive parents. Their club, their rules.)

Your interest in genealogy may be more of a matter of life and death. When we see a new doctor, we are asked to provide a medical history of our family so that the doctor can determine what illnesses are most likely to occur with us due to family genetics. This allows our doctor to suggest lifestyle changes and medical treatments that can prolong our lives even before the earliest symptoms of problems arise. But this means that we need to know as much as possible about illnesses and possible causes of death of our parents, siblings, aunts, uncles, cousins, grandparents, and other relatives. That means doing some research if we don't already know.

What makes us who we are is not only genetics, but also our life experiences, including the aspects of culture passed down to us by our parents. Language, food, music, religion, and countless other large and small bits of culture help to create us as unique individuals, but we may wonder where all these bits originated. Who am I? Where do I come from? These questions can be answered, at least in part, by learning more about the generations that came before us.

Finally, we often engage in genealogy because it is fun. It's mentally challenging, like a good crossword puzzle. But unlike the crossword puzzle that isn't connected to us personally, the same crossword puzzle that may be attempted by millions of other people who see it in the same newspaper, our genealogical puzzle is very personal. It's about us, *only* us. Nobody else, except for our full siblings, has the same set of ancestors, and the same set of genealogical puzzles to solve. Unlike a crossword puzzle, the story created by genealogical research has no definite end. It's a story that needs to be constructed from scratch, and once constructed, told to others so that it can live on, even after we ourselves are gone.

Who was she?

At the beginning of this introduction, I promised you that I would reveal the answer to the mystery of the identity of my Aunt Annie Mae. I learned through standard genealogical research techniques that her married name was Annie Mae King, and that she was the wife (later widow) of Walter King, one of my Grandmother Martin's brothers, who had died almost three years before I was born. So, Aunt Annie Mae King was my great-aunt by marriage. End of story? Does this mean that Aunt Annie Mae wasn't even my blood relative? Not so fast.

You see, I also learned that Aunt Annie Mae King was born Annie Mae Betts, daughter of Lewis B. Betts and Eliza Emma Martin. Martin? Yes. Eliza Emma Martin was *Granddaddy* Martin's half-sister (they had the same father but two different mothers). That meant that Aunt Annie Mae was my blood relative after all! And her children with Walter King and those children's descendants were related to me in two different ways: one way through Granddaddy Martin and the other way through Grandmother Martin. (It happens.) The diagram on the next page may make all of this a little bit clearer.

In the next few chapters, we'll learn the language needed to talk about these sometimes-confusing relationships, and some tools needed to display them so that we can see the relationships at a glance. But we'll start with a fairy tale.

                                        Lewis B. Betts – Eliza Emma Martin
                                                | (half-sister to George Martin,
               (sister and brother) | making her my half-great aunt)
               | | |
George Martin - Lizzie King   **Walter King - Annie Mae Betts**
(my maternal grandparents)   (my great-uncle and his wife,
               | who is also my half-first cousin once removed)
        Corinne Martin
        (my mother)

Part I

For All Generations: Preparing to Research

Chapter 1:
Names, Places, Dates, and Events

Once upon a time, in a land far, far away, there lived …

You may recognize those words as the opening lines of pretty much every fairy tale that has ever been written. It might have continued "a boy/girl/prince/princess named" or "two sisters/two brothers/a sister and a brother named" or in one particular case, "a poor old woodcarver named Geppetto." But no matter how the fairy tale started, it began by saying something about the when, the where, and the who, and then it went on with a bunch of details as to the what (the events of the fairy tale).

Real history is a lot like fairy tales, except that the names refer to real people, the places refer to real locations somewhere on the Earth (or in the case of the Apollo program, on or near the Moon), and the times refer to real years, months, and days according to somebody's calendar. Historians aren't the only ones who care about the who, where, and when. Newspaper journalists also are taught the importance of getting the details of the names, places, and dates when they write the news.

Why is it so important for historical and newspaper stories to pin down the names, places, and dates? Because the events (the what) that make up the rest of the story only make sense in context. Those events are usually related to other events that are happening in or near that same place at or near that same time, and that are happening to one or more people who themselves have a history of events.

New genealogists quickly discover that names, places, and dates are more complicated than they might seem at first glance. Let's look at each of these things, so that we can prepare for these complications.

Names - Part 1: Surnames

Think about the parts of a name. We have given names (also called *first names*) and surnames (also called *family names* or *last names*). In most of the world, we are used to the given name being listed first and the surname being listed last, but there are places where it's the reverse (especially in East Asia and in parts of Eastern Europe, such as Hungary, Albania, and Romania).

Most people in Europe (and their descendants in the New World) would have had surnames at least by the 1600s, but there are exceptions. Eastern European and German Jews were forced by government policies to adopt family names in the late 1700s and early 1800s. And in some places today (Iceland, Myanmar, Java, and parts of East Africa), family names still aren't used.

Speaking of Iceland, let's take a very brief detour to discuss the origin of most European surnames, especially those eventually passed down to their American descendants. When surnames were first adopted, it was certainly common for people to take surnames based on their occupations (miller, smith, farmer, etc.), where they lived (hill, meadows, rivers, etc.), or personal characteristics such as what they looked like or what they wore (short, brown, gray, etc.).

But it was also common for a man to take a surname based on the first name of his father. This system is referred to as *patronymics*. In England and Wales, for example: Johnson, son of John. Williams, son of William. Jones, son of Jone (a spelling of John). Wilson, son of Will. This meant that the surname would change every generation! Eventually, European countries adopted fixed surnames by law, although some of the last holdouts were the Scandinavian countries. You may find an ancestral pair of brothers who emigrated from Scandinavia to the United States with two different surnames: one left Scandinavia before the law, one after! The law would eventually mandate sticking with a particular surname, although depending upon the customs of the region, the name that the family stuck with could have been a patronymic, the name of a farm where the family lived and worked, or another name of choice.

Bottom line: As you do genealogical research, you will expect to find that your ancestors will have a surname in the written records, although you could get back to a time before surnames were even used!

Shakespeare is famous for writing "What's in a name? That which we call a rose by any other name would smell as sweet" in his play *Romeo and Juliet*. Romeo's Montague family was feuding with Juliet's Capulet family. The point of the famous line spoken by Juliet about Romeo is that his being a Montague wasn't important to her: In her opinion, Romeo could change his name and it wouldn't change who he really was.

Some of our ancestors must have taken Juliet's advice, as they frequently changed the spelling of their names, or took on entirely new names. For most of history, people were free to use whatever names they wanted to use, without going through any legal process. Under current U.S. law, except in a few states, people can simply start using a new name, although they would probably have to go through a legal process to get the government or a bank to recognize the change.

We may be used to the idea of married women taking on the surnames of their husbands, but even before the modern era, there were cultures where women kept their birth names (also called *maiden names*), including Malaysia, Korea, and several European countries.

In our modern computerized world, we find name changes to be unusual and even difficult. It wasn't always so. Because it was legal, people could simply stop using one surname and start using another. Perhaps they were moving to a new place and wanted to make a fresh start. Perhaps they saw themselves as the victims of discrimination if they continued to use their existing surname, and they wanted to fit in better with their community. Perhaps they had a falling-out with relatives and didn't want to be associated with their relatives' surname. Perhaps they had a run-in with the law or with someone they owned a debt to. Or perhaps they just liked the new surname because it represented someone they honored or wanted to be associated with. We may never learn the exact reasons why some of our ancestors changed their surnames, but some did.

My great-grandfather Louis Weinglass had a brother, Harris, who had several sons. At least two of those sons changed their surname from Weinglass (pronounced "wine glass") to Wein (which they pronounced "ween"). Why? To fit in? To minimize discrimination against their being Jews? Who knows?

In the pre-computer world, the exact spelling of surnames wasn't as important as it is today, and there was no system for maintaining consistency of spelling. On top of that, our ancestors were not always literate, and while they could pronounce their surname, they may have had no idea how it should be spelled. They depended on record keepers to listen to their name and spell it as they heard it.

My great-grandmother Jane Bodie (pronounced *body* at least until the 1930s) was the descendant of people who spelled the name *Boddie*. I often joke that my South Carolina Bodie ancestors were simply too poor to afford the second "d"! (Their North Carolina cousins kept the Boddie spelling.)

This brings up a very important point: Just because an ancestral family spelled their surname differently from the way your family does, that doesn't indicate that you and they are not related. As the descendant of a Bodie, I am still related to those who spell it Boddie, and probably to those who spell it Boddy, Body, Boddey, Boddye, and . . . well, you get the idea. Never make the mistake of some beginning genealogists who reject a record as not being about their family just because the surname has a different spelling.

Because surnames are normally passed down from father to children, a particular surname is unlikely to be passed to the next generation if a father's children are all daughters. As a result, we sometimes talk about a surname *daughtering out* when there are no more male descendants who carry the surname at some point. In the United States, this means that many unusual surnames are likely to daughter out in the coming years, although the total number of different surnames may continue to increase due to immigration from other countries.

See Figure 1.1 on the next page for a list of common surnames in the United States.

Names - Part 2: Given names

While surnames are also called *family names* because they are automatically handed down through birth into families, *given names* are called that because individuals receive them from their parents. (For those who go through Christian baptism soon after birth, their given name may be referred to as their *Christian name*.)

You may be wondering why I haven't yet mentioned middle names. In the modern world, it's common for everyone to have both a first name and a middle name for their given names, and a few people have multiple middle names. But I've certainly known people who had no middle name. Once populations increased, and more than one person was born having the same given names and surnames, then middle names became a lot more important to distinguish people from each other. Many men, and some women, received their mother's birth surname as their middle name, providing a way to recognize the mother's family. If there were multiple children, then their middle names may have been derived from the names of parents, grandparents, aunts, uncles, or other relatives. Or those middle names may have simply been other names that their parents liked.

So, what are the problems here facing genealogists? The first problem is that you might have two different people who have both the same given name(s) and same surname, living in the same place at about the same time. This means that as you are looking through the records for your own ancestor,

Top 15 Most Popular Last Names in the U.S. by Rank

1990	2000	2010
Smith	Smith	Smith
Johnson	Johnson	Johnson
Williams	Williams	Williams
Jones	Brown	Brown
Brown	Jones	Jones
Davis	Miller	Garcia
Miller	Davis	Miller
Wilson	Garcia	Davis
Moore	Rodriguez	Rodriguez
Taylor	Wilson	Martinez
Anderson	Martinez	Hernandez
Thomas	Anderson	Lopez
Jackson	Taylor	Gonzalez
White	Thomas	Wilson
Harris	Hernandez	Anderson

Figure 1.1: The 15 most common surnames in the U.S. census since 1990 (Source: United States Census Bureau)

you run the risk of confusing that other person with your same-named ancestor. It can be very difficult to separate out one or two (or more) different people with the same name who just happen to share the same place and time as your ancestor.

The next problem is that our ancestors could be very inconsistent about how their given names appeared in the records. They might use a first name in one record, a middle name in another. They might use initials instead. They might use a nickname. Are "William", "Henry", "W.H.", "Will", "Willy", "Willie", "Bill", "Billy", "Billie", and "Hank" all the same man? Are "Amanda", "Manda", and "Mandy" all the same woman? As with surnames, you can't rule out a record as referring to your ancestor just because the given name was slightly different or spelled differently.

In Figure 1.2 below, you can see which first names have been most popular in the United States during the last 100 years. You are very likely to have a lot of ancestors and other relatives with these first names.

Popular names for births in 1920-2019

Rank	Males		Females	
	Name	Number	Name	Number
1	James	4,735,694	Mary	3,265,105
2	John	4,502,387	Patricia	1,560,897
3	Robert	4,499,901	Jennifer	1,467,664
4	Michael	4,330,025	Linda	1,448,309
5	William	3,601,719	Elizabeth	1,428,981
6	David	3,563,170	Barbara	1,402,428
7	Richard	2,467,544	Susan	1,104,407
8	Joseph	2,352,889	Jessica	1,045,519
9	Thomas	2,160,330	Sarah	993,847
10	Charles	2,106,078	Karen	985,728

Figure 1.2: The 10 most popular given names for male and female babies born since 1920 based on Social Security card applications (Source: United States Social Security Administration)

Names - Part 3: Suffixes – Junior and Senior

Some of our ancestors may have had *Junior* (*Jr.*) or *Senior* (*Sr.*) as part of their name. We might refer to this as a *suffix*. Don't assume that a Junior was necessarily the son of a Senior. (I say *son* because it is very rare for women to use the Junior suffix.) In the earlier parts of history, the Junior and Senior labels could be applied to any two men living in the same place at the same time with the same name where one was older than the other. Today, it would be unusual for a Junior not to be the son of a Senior, but you could still find the Roman numerals (II, III, IV, and so forth) used to indicate later descendants with the same name as an older relative, even when the earlier one is not the father of the later one.

Names - Part 4: Prefixes – Medical, religious, and military

The last thing we should learn about names (at least for now) is that some individuals had titles that often accompanied their names and which appeared just before the given name (or just before the surname if the given name wasn't indicated). We can refer to these as a *prefix*. Technically, we could include such titles as "Mr.", "Mrs.", "Miss", and "Ms", but we don't normally record these as we have other places in our software to indicate sex and marital status.

What we often record are "Dr." (whether medical or indicating a non-medical doctoral degree), "Rev." (as well as many other possible religious titles), and abbreviated prefixes for military ranks (Adm., Cpt., Lt., Maj., and Sgt., just to name a few examples). Your genealogy software will normally provide you with a place to enter any prefixes. See Figure 1.3 on the next page for an example.

Names - Part 5: Best practices for recording names

In Chapter 4, we'll discuss genealogy software, but at this point, we need to talk about how you're going to record the names of your ancestors so that you can most easily keep track of them. If a particular ancestor always used the same given names and surname and never changed the spellings, it's easy.

But if the records show different surnames or different spellings of the same name, what do you do? I usually settle on the surname (and its spelling) that I find is most common for that ancestor. Then I can put the alternative spellings (or surnames) in my software's AKA (also known as) or Alternative Name fact, or in the software's Notes field for that ancestor. See Figure 1.4 for an example.

I enter their given names (the first name and, if any, one or more middle names) into the Given name field (or "First and middle name" field, or whatever the software calls this field) and the most common nickname into the Nickname field (other nicknames can go into a Notes field). If your ancestor never went by their first name and always went by their middle name, put that into the Notes field.

Note that some genealogy software may not use different fields for the different parts of a name, but instead will just use one large field for the entire name. This means that the software is assuming that the last word is the surname. This isn't usually a problem unless the surname is a two-part name (such as one starting with "Van"). So be sure to study your software's instructions on how to deal with this.

Add Person
Add a new unlinked person

Given	
Surname	
Prefix	
Suffix	
Nickname	
Sex	Unknown
Living	☑

Figure 1.3: Add Person input screen for RootsMagic 8. Notice the fields for Prefix, Suffix, and Nickname.

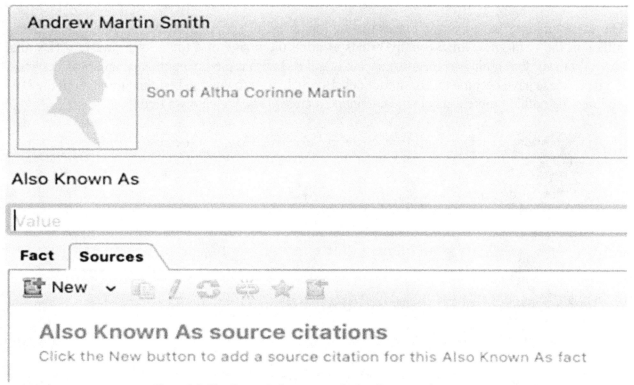

Andrew Martin Smith

Son of Altha Corinne Martin

Also Known As

Value

Fact | **Sources**

📇 New ⌄

Also Known As source citations

Click the New button to add a source citation for this Also Known As fact

Figure 1.4: Also Known As input screen for Family Tree Maker 2019.

Places - Part 1: Place names that changed

"No matter where you go, there you are." That particular sentiment was popularized in 1984 by the movie *The Adventures of Buckaroo Banzai Across the 8th Dimension.* We can use it to remind ourselves that our ancestors frequently moved from place to place, perhaps from the Old World to the New World, or within North America, from country to country or state to state (and between counties within the same state). Genealogical research involves recording these moves over the generations.

But places, like names, bring their own types of complexities. Just as we have learned that our ancestors may have changed their surnames over the generations or used different given names during a single lifetime, we will discover that places have gone by different names over their history. West Virginia was part of Virginia until the 1861–1863 time frame (see Figure 1.5 below). The Province of Carolina in British America was part of the Colony and Dominion of Virginia until 1663, and then split into the Province of North Carolina and the Province of South Carolina in 1729. The town of Greenville, South Carolina, was known as Pleasantburg prior to 1831.

Our ancestors may have lived in places that no longer exist. You've probably heard of ghost towns, although the term *ghost town* usually brings to mind the image of a town in the western U.S. that thrived during the mining of metals (especially gold), but that died once the resource was depleted. Some of these have become tourist attractions. But real ghost towns can be found throughout the U.S. and may be nothing more today than an unmarked crossroads. How do we find them?

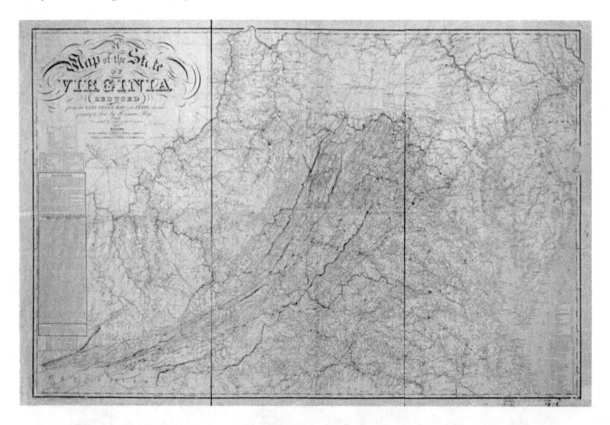

Figure 1.5: This 1859 map shows West Virginia as part of Virginia. (Source: Library of Congress)

Places - Part 2: Finding places

If you know that your ancestors lived in a big city such as Newark, New Jersey, you aren't going to have much trouble finding it on a modern map. But how do you locate those tiny places that might not even exist today (or that may have had their names changed since your ancestors lived there)? I usually start by searching the Geographic Names Information System (GNIS). The GNIS is a service of the United States Geological Survey (USGS), a scientific bureau of the U.S. Department of the Interior. The USGS worked with the U.S. Board on Geographic Names (BGN), which is responsible for standardizing the names of all kinds of places within the U.S. By using the GNIS, you can check a place name that you've discovered to see exactly where it is (or was), and then see what is at that location on a modern map. The GNIS contains information about more than two million names, including names for populated places, bodies of water, cemeteries, and churches.

Unfortunately, the BGN announced on October 27, 2021, that they were going to archive a number of categories of places, which they call *features*: Airport, Bridge, Building, Cemetery, Church, Dam, Forest, Harbor, Hospital, Mine, Oilfield, Park, Post Office, Reserve, School, Tower, Trail, Tunnel, and Well. It appears that these kinds of places will be made available only as downloadable files and will not be searchable through the usual means. Fortunately, you will still be able to search for populated places and for natural places (such as bodies of water).

See Figure 1.6 for an example of what the GNIS query form looks like. To read more about the GNIS (and to find the link to "Search Domestic Names", go to:
www.usgs.gov/core-science-systems/ngp/board-on-geographic-names/domestic-names

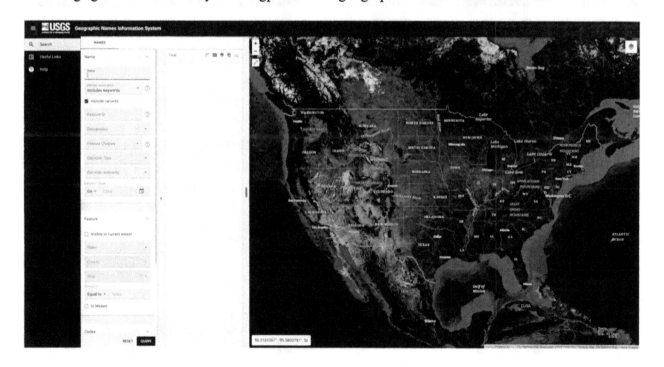

Figure 1.6: USGS Geographic Names Information System (GNIS) query form (Source: United States Department of the Interior)

You're not out of the woods yet (pardon the geographic pun). Just as we saw with the names of people, where two or more people living in the same place at the same time could have the same name, we may learn that two or more populated places in the same state (and even in the same county) could have the same name. Searching the GNIS for Salem, South Carolina, as the name of a populated place, I find four different populated places named "Salem" (two of them in Florence County), two different places named "Salem Crossroads", one "Salem Estates", one "Salem Plantation", one "New Salem", and one "Ole Salem Estates". If one of my ancestors was said to have lived in Salem, how will I know which one it was?

This is where historical maps come in. I happen to own printed copies of county maps for some of the locations where my ancestors lived (remember, I got started with genealogical research nearly 30 years ago when online research wasn't really a thing), but today it isn't generally necessary for you to buy copies of historical maps. You will find that many historical maps for the United States (all the way back to colonial times when it was British America) and for other parts of the world have been scanned and put online to be browsed at your convenience.

Start by visiting the David Rumsey Map Collection Database (davidrumsey.com) and the University of Texas Libraries' Map Collection (maps.lib.utexas.edu). (See Figure 1.7 below and Figure 1.8 on the next page.)

Figure 1.7: David Rumsey Map Collection home page (Source: davidrumsey.com)

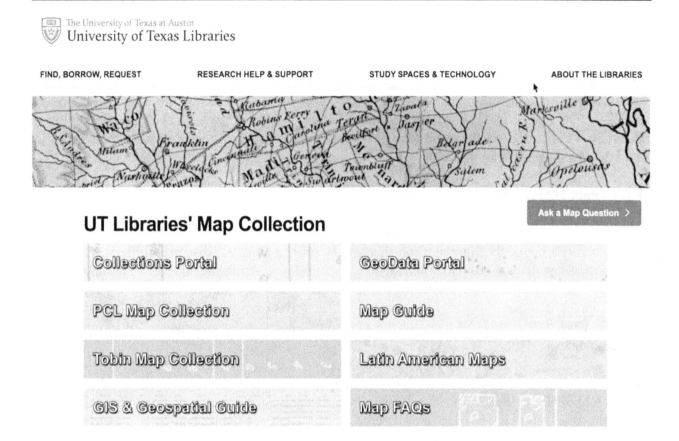

Figure 1.8: University of Texas Libraries' Map Collection (Source: University of Texas Libraries)

Then visit the map collections at the Library of Congress (loc.gov/maps) and the National Archives and Records Administration (archives.gov/research/cartographic). Another method is to use Google to look for "historical map" together with the place name of interest.

Places - Part 3: Best practices for recording places

When entering places into your genealogical software, use all of the necessary geographic divisions to be clear as to which place it is: Newberry, Newberry County, South Carolina, United States. It's a personal decision as to whether to include the word "County" (or "Parish" for Louisiana), and whether to include "United States." Whatever you decide, remember to be consistent throughout all of your research. It's also possible that your software will allow you to enter the place in different ways (a usual way, a standardized way, and an abbreviated way).

What if the place has a different name today or is now in a different county or state? Experts may disagree (and I'll explain why), but I recommend that you use the name of the place as it was when the ancestral event (birth, marriage, death, etc.) occurred. This means that you use "Virginia", not "West Virginia," for events that took place prior to 1861–1863. You can use the Notes field to indicate that the place would be in West Virginia today.

Some experts always use the modern name because it may allow the software more easily to display the location on a modern map. However, I don't think that genealogists should change their practices

17

just to accommodate the limitations of genealogical software. Instead, we should request that software be upgraded to know the beginning and ending dates of when geographic places existed.

Be careful never to make assumptions about places. For instance, if you know only the U.S. state as a certainty, but not the county, then don't enter the county (you can mention the county in the Notes field if you have some idea). You may want to include *near* or *nr* as part of a place description if you have reason to believe that the event took place near (but not in) a particular place, or indicate in the notes that the actual location is "near."

Dates - Part 1: Our Gregorian calendar

In the classic Lerner and Loewe song "I Remember It Well" from the 1958 movie *Gigi*, an older man and woman (portrayed by Maurice Chevalier and Hermione Gingold) disagree on the details of the story of their last rendezvous. One remembers it as a Friday in April, the other as a Monday in June. This entertaining song serves as a warning to genealogists about how human memory can be extremely fallible, including when it comes to remembering dates. But even if the records of historical events agree on what date it was, we can still run into some unexpected problems with determining and recording dates.

We may think of the calendar as unchanging, except for that pesky 29 February inserted every four years. Our popular calendar, officially known as the Gregorian calendar, is the one most used around the world, at least for civil (non-religious) purposes. But it has not always existed, and there are many other calendars still in use today besides the Gregorian one. If you have Jewish ancestors, you may already be familiar with the Hebrew calendar. Other calendars include the Islamic calendar and several different East Asian calendars, such as Chinese, Japanese, Korean, and Thai.

The Gregorian calendar first came into existence in October 1582, introduced to the world by Pope Gregory XIII, so he gets his name on it. (See Figure 1.9 on the next page for an example of a 1582 historical Gregorian calendar.) As a result, it was adopted by most Catholic populations almost immediately, but not by Protestant or Eastern Orthodox countries until much later. Greece, a predominantly Eastern Orthodox country, didn't start using the Gregorian calendar until 1923!

The Gregorian calendar was a replacement for the Julian calendar, which had been in use in Europe since the days of Julius Caesar and the Roman Empire. For those of us with ancestors who lived in British America, we must deal with the Julian calendar because the Parliament of Great Britain waited until 1750 to pass an act that switched Britain and its colonies to the Gregorian calendar in 1752. So, what happened to make the switch possible? Several things, and it's complicated.

First, under the previous calendar, the first day of the year was 25 March, celebrated by many Christians as Lady Day. Under the new calendar, the first day of the year moved to 1 January. This means that 1751 was the shortest year in British history, starting with 25 March and ending with 31 December (only 282 days).

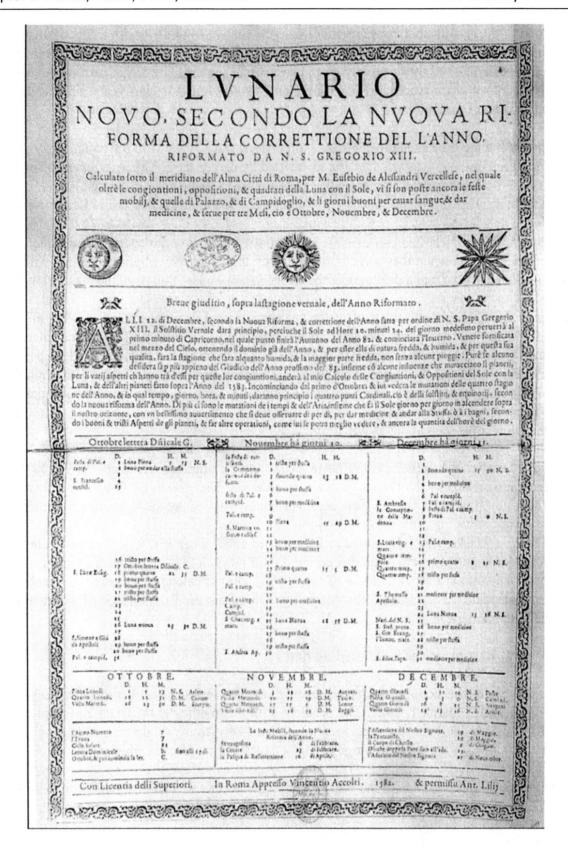

Figure 1.9: A 1582 printed edition of the new Gregorian calendar. (Source: The Vatican Library)

Second, one of the reasons that Pope Gregory made the change from the existing Julian calendar was that adding a leap day every four years (without exception) made the Julian calendar get out of kilter with the solar calendar (all those equinoxes and solstices). The new Gregorian calendar added a rule saying that century years (such as 1700, 1800, and 1900) were not leap years, unless they were divisible by 400 (such as 1600 and 2000).

Although this change prevented the calendar from drifting out of sync with the natural seasons, there was still the problem that the dates had already drifted by eleven days. This was remedied by having Wednesday, 2 September 1752, be immediately followed by Thursday, 14 September 1752. That's right, folks: In the British Empire, the dates 3 September 1752 to 13 September 1752 never existed!

For genealogical purposes, this can cause a bit of confusion. If you are trying to calculate how old someone was based on when they were born and when they died, you might be dealing with a birth under the Julian calendar and a death under the Gregorian calendar. You could be off by eleven days!

Additional confusion is due to the start of the year becoming 1 January instead of 25 March. Dates between 1 January and 25 March would be in two different years depending on which calendar you were using. Under the Julian calendar (known as *Old Style* or *OS*), the date would be part of the previous year, while under the Gregorian calendar (known as *New Style* or *NS*), the date would be part of the current year. As a result, you may see genealogical records using a system of "dual dating" (or "double dating"), where the year is given as two years with a slash between, letting you know that the first one is OS and the second one is NS.

As mentioned earlier, the Catholic countries tended to switch much earlier, so any records in the New World that were created by the French or the Spanish would likely be in the Gregorian calendar after 1582. You might think, then, that all New World calendars were under the Gregorian system by 1752.

But then there's Alaska, which belonged to Russia until 1867, when it was sold to the United States. Russia, a predominantly Eastern Orthodox country, didn't switch to the Gregorian calendar until after the October Revolution of 1917. So, 7 October 1867 (Julian calendar) became 18 October 1867 (Gregorian calendar). At the same time, Alaska switched from the Russian side of the International Date Line to the American side.

Dates - Part 2: Best practices for recording dates

In the United States it is common to record recent dates as a series of numbers separated by slashes, such as 03/01/22 for March 1, 2022. The problem with this method (MM/DD/YY) is that it can be very confusing for those in Europe, who are more likely to write the same date as 01/03/22 (DD/MM/YY). What's the solution for genealogists, who want to avoid ambiguity?

First, we're going to be writing out the year as four digits, so that we can easily distinguish 2022 from 1922, 1822, and so forth. Second, we're going to use words, not numbers, for the months. You can abbreviate the month in three letters (some genealogy software can do this automatically for you). Finally, we'll start with the date, then have the month, and lastly the year. This gives us: 1 March 2022 (or 1 Mar 2022).

Events

If a story was nothing more than names, places, and dates, it wouldn't even be a story. A real story is about what happens to those people in those places on those dates. What are the details of their lives? In genealogy, we are interested in our ancestors' births, marriages, and deaths. We want to know about their military service, occupations, education, migration from one place to another, religious affiliations, legal actions, and whatever else we can learn about them.

Typical genealogy software provides us with dozens of different types of facts that we can use to describe the lives of our ancestors. And the software may give us the option of customized facts for more unusual events that the software couldn't predict in advance.

When we have dates for the events in our ancestors' lives, we are then able to create a timeline for them. We can see how their lives developed, one event after another.

In later chapters, we'll look at the details of these life events, and the records that they leave behind.

Chapter 2: Relationships

Any time you take on a new hobby, interest, or profession, you know that there are going to be new concepts to learn. These concepts may use terms that you've never seen before, or they may use old words in new or very precise ways. It's no different with genealogy. In this chapter, we'll learn about the concepts that deal with how two people are related to each other.

Names for relationships

Before you decided to adopt genealogy as a hobby or profession, you already knew some basic family relationship terms:

Father
Mother
Parent
Husband
Wife
Spouse
Son
Daughter
Child (in the sense of son or daughter, not in the sense of pre-adult)
Brother
Sister
Sibling
Grandfather
Grandmother
Grandparent
Grandson
Granddaughter
Grandchild
In-law (including *father-in-law*, *mother-in-law*, *son-in-law*, *daughter-in-law*, *brother-in-law*, and *sister-in-law*)

Good news! Genealogy is not going to change the meanings of those words.

(By the way, in some cultures, many of the terms in the above list or the terms discussed below are also used for non-relatives as terms of endearment or as forms of respect. Nobody, certainly not me, is suggesting that you stop doing that. Just be careful when you are using those terms around other genealogists to avoid confusion.)

Things start getting a little bit trickier when we move to some other terms that you already use, but which genealogists need to be very careful with:

Aunt
Uncle

Outside of genealogy, we use words like *aunt* and *uncle* to refer not only to the siblings of our parents, but also to the spouses of those siblings (your parents' sisters-in-law and brothers-in-law). In genealogy, we want to be careful to distinguish these different kinds of relationships. In ordinary conversation, you don't have to start referring to the wife of your Uncle John as *Aunt-in-law Mary* or the husband of your Aunt Laura as *Uncle-by-marriage Joe*, but in genealogy (when you're talking to another genealogist), it's probably best if you referred to her as *Uncle John's wife* and to him as *Aunt Laura's husband.*

Niece
Nephew

In the same way, a married couple will usually call all the children of their siblings' *niece* or *nephew*, even if they are the children of their sisters-in-law or brothers-in-law. This is the *Aunt* and *Uncle* problem from the other end. In genealogy, we want to be clear that Sue and Bob are John's niece and nephew, but Mary's niece and nephew only by marriage.

Step

Thanks to fairy tales, step relatives have gotten a bad reputation. Perhaps the *Brady Bunch* was able to undo some of that unfortunate publicity. But remarriages among parents do result in new legal relationships between parents and children, or among children. As genealogists, we need to keep track of step relatives (trust me on this for now), whether they are stepmothers, stepfathers, stepsisters, stepbrothers, stepdaughters, or stepsons. When discussing my own family tree, I've had to use words like step-grandmother and step-grandson to be crystal clear about their relationships, although these terms are not common.

However, I am not telling you that you can't or shouldn't refer to your stepparent as *Mom* or *Dad* or to your stepchild as *my daughter* or *my son*. The language we choose to use within our own families is important for expressions of love and respect.

What I *am* telling you is that you need to use careful language when you are discussing or writing genealogy, so that the listener or reader understands the exact relationship being described.

Half

If the Brady parents had added new babies to the family, those children would have been half-siblings (half-sisters or half-brothers) to the six existing Brady kids. Half-siblings share one parent instead of two. This means that you could have a half-aunt or half-uncle (the half-sibling to one of your parents) and they can have half-nieces and half-nephews.

Great and grand

Grandmothers and grandfathers (grandparents) are no mystery. Neither are granddaughters and grandsons (grandchildren). That's why I put those words on the first list.

Once you get back (or forward) to another generation, we add the word *great*. This gives us great-grandmothers and great-grandfathers (great-grandparents) and great-granddaughters and great-grandsons (great-grandchildren).

We keep adding *great* for each generation back, but as you might imagine, this is going to make for some very long words. So, genealogists usually resort to numbers, such as *2g-grandparent* or *3g-grandchild*. In that way, we don't have to write *great-great* or *great-great-great*.

Okay, it's time to introduce some controversy into this book. What should you call the person who is the sister of your grandparent? Great-aunt? Grandaunt (with or without a hyphen)? And the person who is the brother of your grandparent? Great-uncle? Granduncle (with or without a hyphen)? Answer: Whichever you like. It's personal preference. One form is not more "technically correct" than the other. Don't let anyone tell you different (and trust me, they will try). Both forms of these words have existed as part of the English language for hundreds of years. As a genealogist, pick the one you like and stick with it (consistency is a virtue in genealogy), but be prepared to read and understand the form you don't personally use, and please don't try to "correct" the other person for using it.

Cousin

I must admit that I saved this one for last, because it is the most complicated and the one that confuses many genealogists, especially beginners. Non-genealogists pretty much call any relative a "cousin" who doesn't fit into one of the previously described relationships. They don't have to worry about the details. As a genealogist, you do. Sorry, but I'm not going to let you throw up your hands at this point and say "I just call 'em all 'cousins'." Nope, you can learn this. Here we go:

The children of our aunts and uncles are our *first cousins*. Put another way, first cousins are individuals who share the same set of grandparents. (Half-first cousins share a single grandparent.)

The children of your first cousins are not your second cousins. (Repeat that statement to yourself as many times as you need to. In the non-genealogical world, folks don't believe it.) *Second cousins* share the same set of great-grandparents. You and your second cousins are at the same generational level, just as you and your first cousins are. And this means...

Third cousins share the same set of 2g-grandparents. And *fourth cousins* share the same set of 3g-grandparents. And so on, back as many generations as you want to go. (Did you notice that you can subtract one from the number of *g*s in order to figure out what the cousin level is?)

These numbers (first, second, third, and so forth) tell us the *degree* of relationship. Some genealogists refer to any cousins more distant than first cousins as *distant cousins*, while others use the term to refer to any cousin who they don't know personally. (And if you're wondering about the term *kissing cousin*, don't worry; it's not a term you're likely to find in any serious genealogical discussion.)

So, we now have something more exact than cousin to refer to these more distant relatives. Again, if you are in touch with these relatives, feel free to refer to them as Cousin Daniel or Cousin Sofia, even if Daniel is your second cousin and Sofia is your third cousin.

Double Cousins

One more term you may encounter is *double cousin*. Double cousins occur when one pair of siblings marries another pair of siblings. This means that their children are related as first cousins on both sides of their family. (I'll bring this situation up again when we discuss DNA testing in a later chapter.)

Removed

But we've left something undefined. If you can't refer to the children of your first cousins as *second cousins*, how should you refer to them? You're not in the same generation as they are. They are in a generation one generation later. They are *one generation removed* from you. (Insert joke at this point of how you definitely have some relatives who you'd like to remove.)

Thus, if Christopher is your first cousin, then Christopher's children are your first cousins once removed. And Christopher's grandchildren are your first cousins twice removed. If Maria is your second cousin, then Maria's children are your second cousins once removed. And Maria's grandchildren are your second cousins twice removed.

And these *removed* relationships work in both generational directions exactly the same. Your own parents' first cousins are your first cousins once removed. And your own grandparents' first cousins are your first cousins twice removed. *Removed* cousins can be in a generation earlier than you or in a generation later than you.

Some genealogists use a chart to keep track of these cousin relationships, but I just remind myself: first cousins share grandparents, second cousins share great-grandparents, and so forth, and *removed* just counts the number of generations of difference between you and the cousin.

I won't mind if you feel the need to re-read this section of the book many times over in the years to come.

Visualizing relationships

Genealogists have long used two different methods to display genealogical relationships: the *pedigree chart* (sometimes called an *ancestor chart*) and the *family group sheet* (sometimes called a *family group record*). Let's see what they look like and how they are used.

Pedigree Chart

The word *pedigree* has been part of the English language since at least the 1400s, and it appears to have come into English from Anglo-Norman French, with the idea that a pedigree looks like the foot (*pe*) of (*de*) a crane (*grue*).

The pedigree concept has been used for hundreds of years not only for human beings, but also for domesticated animals bred for particular traits, such as dogs and racehorses. The American Kennel Club (AKC) keeps track of dog pedigrees in the United States, while The Kennel Club (KC) keeps track of them in the United Kingdom. And you've probably heard of the brand of dog food that uses the word *pedigree* in its name. But let's get back to humans and their pedigrees, shall we?

The point of a pedigree chart is to show all of a person's direct ancestors (parents, grandparents, great-grandparents, and so forth) at least as far back as can be easily shown on a single page, usually four to six generations in total. It's possible to extend the chart to additional pages to display older generations, if the research has been done that far back.

By convention, in each generation, the father is listed above the mother. (I'm not aware of any convention for when both legal parents are of the same sex, but it might make sense to list the older of the couple above and the younger below.) The name of each person is usually accompanied by at least their years of birth and death, and if there is room, the chart may include their exact birth dates and death dates, as well as birth locations, death locations, and marriage dates and locations.

Genealogists like pedigree charts because they provide a great visualization of many people on a single page, showing exactly how someone (you, for instance) is related to some distant ancestor. Beginners may want to start with a paper pedigree chart (and a pencil with a good eraser) as they start their ancestral journey, to help them learn who goes where. See Figure 2.1 on the next page for an example of a filled-in pedigree chart.

Family Group Sheet

Nearly one hundred years ago, the genealogical arm of The Church of Jesus Christ of Latter-day Saints, then known as the Genealogical Society of Utah (GSU) but now known as FamilySearch, introduced to its church members a new way of recording family information on a single page. (I'll discuss the relationship between the Church and genealogy in a later chapter.) This new record format, usually called a *family group sheet*, allowed for the display of a set of parents and all of their children (and possibly their spouses), together with the details of their birth, marriage, and death dates and locations. See Figure 2.2 on page 27 for an example of a filled-in family group sheet.

Figure 2.1: Filled-in pedigree chart using RootsMagic 8

Family of George Washington Martin and Elizabeth Estelle "Lizzie" King

FATHER George Washington Martin

	BIRTH	12 Jan 1882	Edgefield, South Carolina, United States
	DEATH	12 Nov 1964	Newberry, Newberry, South Carolina, United States

MOTHER Elizabeth Estelle "Lizzie" King

	BIRTH	7 Oct 1884	Laurens, South Carolina, United States
	DEATH	1 Apr 1973	Newberry, Newberry, South Carolina, United States

CHILDREN

M	**Walter Lee Martin**		
	BIRTH	29 Jul 1902	Laurens, Laurens, South Carolina, United States
	DEATH	9 Apr 1989	Laurens, Laurens, South Carolina, United States

M	**George Ernest Martin**		
	BIRTH	19 Jun 1906	South Carolina, United States
	DEATH	27 Apr 1970	Newberry, Newberry, South Carolina, United States

F	**Anna Naomi Martin**		
	BIRTH	31 Jan 1908	Laurens, Laurens, South Carolina, United States
	DEATH	22 Mar 1976	San Diego, San Diego, California, United States

M	**Robert Ansel Martin**		
	BIRTH	8 Jan 1910	Newberry, Newberry, South Carolina, United States
	DEATH	16 Nov 1971	Newberry, Newberry, South Carolina, United States

F	**Mattie Cleo Martin**		
	BIRTH	4 Aug 1912	Newberry, Newberry, South Carolina, United States
	DEATH	18 Mar 2002	San Diego, San Diego, California, United States

F	**Marion Virginia Martin**		
	BIRTH	31 Oct 1918	Chappells, Newberry, South Carolina, United States
	DEATH	14 Jan 1992	Newberry, Newberry, South Carolina, United States

F	**Altha Corinne Martin**		
	BIRTH	19 Dec 1920	Moon Township, Newberry, South Carolina, United States
	DEATH	16 Jun 2007	Newberry, Newberry, South Carolina, United States

Figure 2.2 Filled-in family group sheet using RootsMagic 8

Both the pedigree chart and the family group sheet are a standard part of genealogical research. By using these tools, you can quickly see what information you already have and what information may be missing. Genealogy software will offer the ability to display or print your information in both of these formats, and we'll talk about this kind of software in Chapter 4.

Chapter 3:
The Genealogical Research Process

At this point, you know that your genealogical research will give you the ability to construct stories about your ancestors, with details about the events of their lives: the names, places, and dates. It will allow you to figure out how each of your ancestors is related to you and how they are related to each other, and you'll be able to name these relationships and visualize them on pedigree charts and family group sheets.

But how do you actually do the research? Research of any kind is a process, and genealogical research shares a lot of similarities with other kinds of research—even the kind that you may have experienced while writing a research paper in high school or college. If you obtained a graduate degree and had to write a thesis or dissertation, some of what follows is going to sound especially familiar. Don't worry, whether or not you've ever done research of any type, or if it has been a very long time since you last did, we'll go carefully through each of the steps, and you'll be fine!

Define your research goal

Research of any type is only successful when there is a research goal. By a research goal, I mean the thing that you want to achieve by doing the research. For instance, my surname is Smith, and a valid research goal for me would be to trace my Smith ancestors back in time for as far as I can go. Genealogists often adopt a goal of focusing on one particular surname in their family and seeing how far back they can go with it.

Another goal might be to fill in all the blanks for your ancestry for several generations back. If you're a beginner genealogist, you might want to figure out who all your grandparents, great-grandparents, and great-great-grandparents are.

Once you have become more experienced, you might want to tackle a more difficult goal. You might have an ancestor who immigrated to the New World in the 1600s or 1700s, and you might choose to work on determining who all their living descendants are. This is a very ambitious research goal, and it's not even a goal that can be completely done, since new descendants can be born every day!

The point of having a research goal before you get started in all of this is that you can use it to figure out how well you are doing and what remains to be done. It keeps you focused on your research. Otherwise, you might meander all over your family tree, and never make much progress with any of it. If that happens, it is disappointing.

Take a moment to think about your own research goal (or goals; you're encouraged to have two or three, but don't go crazy) and write it down somewhere. Write it on a whiteboard or print it out and tack it to a cork board. Even better, make it your computer's screen desktop! Having your research goal in front of you is a good way to stay motivated as you sit down to do genealogy.

By the way: It's ok if you get into your research and change your mind later about your research goal. You may decide that you chose a goal that was too ambitious or that no longer interests you. If so, don't feel stuck. Change the goal, and then commit yourself to your new goal.

The Genealogical Proof Standard (GPS)

If you were to ask a non-genealogist what "GPS" meant, they would likely assume that you were talking about the Global Positioning System, the U.S. government's satellite-based navigation system, the one that has resulted over the past few decades in the development of in-car directional tools and cool smartphone mapping apps. No more need for paper maps when you're driving or walking from Point A to Point B!

Even genealogists use that particular kind of GPS, but when they do, it's more likely used to pin down the exact location of a gravesite in a cemetery.

But genealogists (especially in the United States) know about another kind of GPS, the one that stands for *Genealogical Proof Standard*. The Board for Certification of Genealogists® (BCG) published a set of standards in 2000 (the *BCG Genealogical Standards Manual*), which has been updated in a second edition revised as of 2021 (*Genealogy Standards*).

Even beginning genealogists (yes, you included) should be familiar with the Genealogical Proof Standard. In its most basic form, it consists of five parts:

- Research (finding all of the relevant sources of information)
- Citation (identifying exactly what each source of information is and where it came from)
- Analysis (looking at the information, understanding what it says, and putting it together with other information)
- Resolving (when you've got contradictory information, how do you handle it?)
- Conclusion (writing down the process by which you decided that the evidence you have leads to a fact about your ancestor that you now believe)

Don't be intimated by the GPS. It's a very useful tool to remind us of the best practices for doing genealogical research. We'll cover each of these five parts in more detail.

Finding sources of information

Types of sources

A large part of this book will be about how you find, understand, and use different types of sources of information that mention your ancestors. These genealogical sources will include things produced by your ancestors themselves (or their relatives, friends, neighbors, and others they interacted with), such as letters and diaries. There will be newspaper articles that mention your ancestors. You'll find government records (such as birth, marriage/divorce, death, census, immigration, land, military, naturalization, probate, retirement, and tax). There may be religious records (baptism/christening, marriage, death/burial, membership) and funeral home and cemetery records. A few things were produced by companies and other organizations, such as school yearbooks, city directories, employment records, and society membership records. Don't worry. We'll cover each of these: how to find them, how to understand them, and how to use them.

Repositories

Sources of genealogical information can exist in many different places. They include:

- Sources found in your own home or in the homes of relatives (we'll get to these in a later chapter)
- Personal memories - your own and those of living relatives (we'll get to these also in a later chapter)
- Physical repositories - archives, courthouses, libraries, and other offices designed to preserve historical records
- Online repositories (websites)

Prior to the development of the Internet, most genealogical information was found only in physical repositories. Even today, trips to repositories are still essential to good genealogical research, whether you go yourself or get someone else to go on your behalf.

Today, we also have the luxury of a great deal of genealogical information being brought directly to our own homes, 24/7, through websites. Some of these are the websites of those same libraries and archives, which have been digitizing portions of their records and putting the digital images online. However, the largest online digital collections can be found at a small number of organizational or commercial websites, including:

- familysearch.org, operated by FamilySearch
- ancestry.com, operated by Ancestry.com
- myheritage.com, operated by MyHeritage
- findmypast.com, operated by Findmypast

It may be a little confusing at first, but genealogists use the names FamilySearch, Ancestry, MyHeritage, and Findmypast sometimes to refer to the websites and sometimes to refer to the organizations/companies that run them. Fortunately, you can usually use context to figure out which one is meant.

In Chapter 7, we'll look into the best ways to use any online repository. In the meantime, let's learn a little bit about "the big four".

FamilySearch

FamilySearch is the non-profit organization that maintains familysearch.org. FamilySearch (the organization) was formerly the Genealogical Society of Utah (GSU), founded in 1894, and is part of The Church of Jesus Christ of Latter-day Saints. FamilySearch (the website) was first made available in 1999. It is free and available to everyone, not just to members of the Church, although a few website features may be restricted to access by Church members only.

FamilySearch lists more than three thousand genealogical record collections, with more than three billion digitized images and eight billion searchable names. The record collections span every inhabited continent of the world but are especially strong in records from the United States, Canada, the United Kingdom and Ireland, Continental Europe, and Latin America.

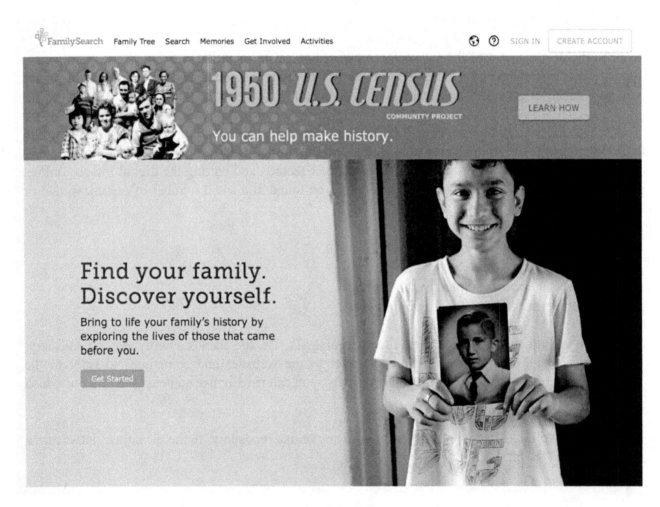

Figure 3.1: FamilySearch home page

Ancestry.com

For non-genealogists, Ancestry.com is undoubtedly the best-known of the large genealogical companies, due to their long-time TV advertising and their sponsorship of such TV shows as the American edition of *Who Do You Think You Are?*. The company got its start in 1983 publishing genealogical magazines and books, but launched its website in 1996, and soon became the largest commercial site for online genealogical information.

Ancestry.com lists more than 33,000 record collections. As with FamilySearch, the Ancestry collections cover the world, but they are especially strong with records from the United States, Canada, Europe, and Australia.

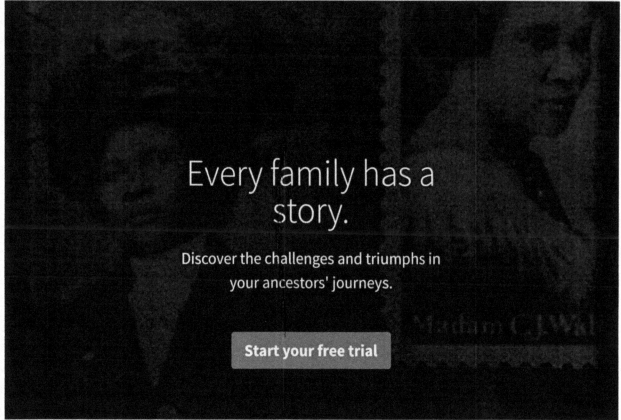

Figure 3.2: Ancestry home page

MyHeritage

MyHeritage was formed in Israel in 2003 and grew quickly as a company by acquiring other existing genealogical companies and their record collections in Germany, Poland, the Netherlands, and France, plus several genealogical family tree websites.

The MyHeritage website lists more than 6,800 record collections containing nearly 18 billion records. MyHeritage has record collections from all inhabited continents but is especially strong with records from the United States and Europe.

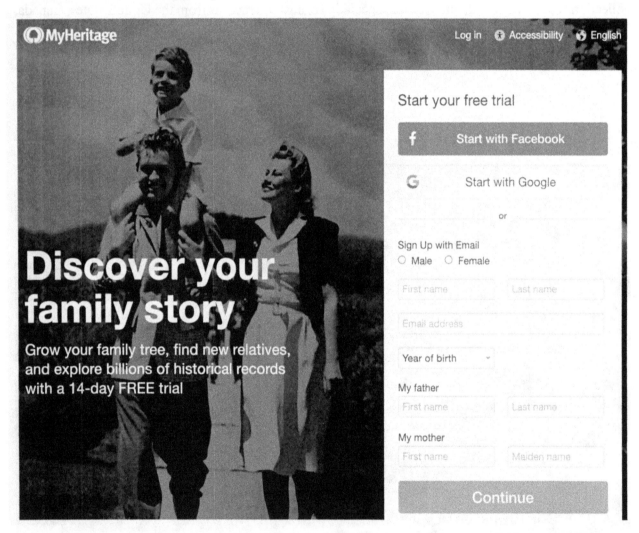

Figure 3.3: MyHeritage home page

Findmypast

Findmypast is a London-based company. Its genealogy website dates back to 2003 under the name 1837online, becoming Findmypast in 2006. Findmypast is now owned by DC Thomson, a Scottish publishing and television production company, and it partners with a number of British and Irish government agencies and organizations.

Findmypast has more than 2,600 record sets, containing more than two billion records. It is especially strong in records from Britain, Ireland, and the United States.

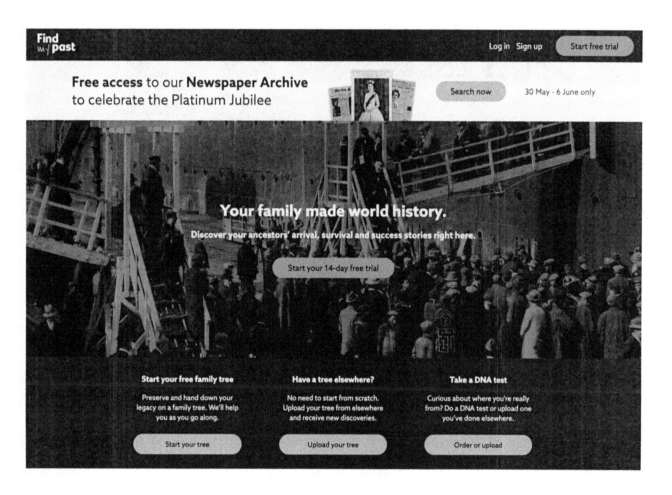

Figure 3.4 Findmypast home page

Other online repositories

There are countless other online genealogical repositories. Smaller than the "big four" previously described, these other sites normally cater to a particular geographical area (such as the northeastern United States) or to a particular ethnic group (such as Jewish or African American). You can use Cyndi's List (cyndislist.com) to find any that are relevant to your genealogical research.

Figure 3.5: Cyndi's List home page

Problems with sources

Historical sources for genealogical research present us with a number of challenges. They may be hard to read, perhaps because the image has faded or because the sources are handwritten and difficult to decipher. They may be in a language we don't speak. They may use terminology that is from an earlier time but that is no longer used or that has changed meanings. This is especially true for legal or medical source documents.

What's worse, we may not be looking at the original sources. In some cases, the original sources may not be easy to get to, or they may have been destroyed. Instead, we may be looking only at a derivative source, such as a transcription, index, or abstract.

Transcriptions are where someone else read the source and wrote down what they thought it said. But this could have introduced errors, especially when it comes to things like names, places, and dates. How can you tell if what you are reading is an original or a transcription? If you're reading typewritten material that is dated prior to the mid-1870s (when typewriters were first introduced into offices), you are looking at a typed transcription of material that was originally handwritten. If you are seeing something strange in the material, such as a page number in the middle of the text, that's a tip-off that the material must have been transcribed from a paginated document.

In a similar way, we may be looking at only an index or an abstract (summary) of the original set of documents. While indexes can be extremely helpful in finding the document we need among hundreds or thousands of pages, they can also introduce errors and cause us to miss a useful document. Abstracts, which are designed to summarize the most useful parts of a document, may overlook some things that we still want to see, and they too can suffer from the introduction of errors.

Bottom line: A good rule for genealogists is to find out if the original source is still available, so that we can compare it with the transcription, index, or abstract to see if errors were made or information was omitted. However, if all we have is a derivative source, we may have to be content with that.

Citing what you find

When we use information for our research, we need to keep track of where we found it. When we wrote papers in high school or college, we were taught to cite our sources. Citing our sources helps us in multiple ways:

First, it lets us (and others) easily go back to the sources to see if they actually say what we think they said. Second, and more importantly, the citations give us (and others) confidence that we looked for the most relevant types of sources for the historical facts we are trying to establish. Years from now, there might be some new genealogical sources that are available that weren't available when we did our original research. If so, our citations will show which sources we used and which ones we may have overlooked or which we may not yet have had access to.

Don't worry, citing genealogical sources is a bit easier than it used to be. Genealogical software provides us with templates that make filling in the information much easier.

Analyzing what you find

Let's say that you've found some information that appears to be about your ancestor, and you've cited it so that you can find it again and figure out what it was and where it came from. You still have a lot of questions you're going to need to ask yourself. This is because:

- The information may not be about your ancestor after all. It might be about another person with the same name, who may have lived in the same place around the same time as your ancestor. How much confidence do you have that you are looking at the right person?
- People are only human. By this, I mean that people produce sources with incorrect information. They may have misremembered, miscopied something from another source, or lied. How much confidence do you have that the information is accurate and honest?
- Smudged typing or difficult handwriting can lead to misinterpretations about what the source says. How much confidence do you have that you are reading the source correctly?

Once you've felt good about addressing these questions, you can now take this source's information and put it together with information from other sources. But this might lead to one additional problem.

Resolving contradictions in your information

Think back to the last time two different friends told you a story about what each of them experienced at the same event. Their two stories might agree on a lot of points but might differ on others. Whose story do you believe? Is one right and the other wrong? Could they both be wrong? Is one (or both) of your friends simply misremembering? Does one of your friends have a better memory than the other? Is one purposely misrepresenting what happened because telling the truth might cause them some embarrassment? Is one of your friends a bit more honest than the other?

When you search for information about your ancestors, you can expect that most of the information you find is going to be consistent with other information. But there is also a good chance that some of it is going to contradict other information. Just as you do when you hear contradictory stories from friends, you are going to have to deal with contradictory genealogical information. And you're going to have to decide how to resolve that so that you can tell a consistent story about your ancestors.

Coming to a conclusion about a genealogical fact

You try to find as many original sources as you can, but you deal with derivative sources if you have to. You cite the sources you find. You analyze the information to figure out what it says. You deal with any contradictions. You are now ready to come up with your conclusion. What do you think is the fact about your ancestor's life, and why do you think it?

Your ancestors were real people living real lives. They had real birth dates and locations, may have had one or more real marriages on real dates and at real locations, and if they are no longer alive, they had real death dates and locations. All of the other things that may have happened to them (church affiliation, migration, military service, and so forth) were real events, too.

Your role, as a genealogist, is to tell the real story about your ancestors, and by following these research steps, you'll have the best chance of discovering the real facts of their lives.

Chapter 4:
Tools and Methods to Keep Us Organized

Computer software and hardware

Once genealogists started to own personal computers in large numbers, software developers knew it was time to create software applications designed specifically for keeping track of genealogical information. Some of the earliest programs appeared in the late 1980s, and today there are at least a dozen popular programs and many, many more that have their own smaller but devoted followings.

Some genealogy programs are Windows-only, some are macOS-only, and some are available for both platforms. Based on what I've seen when people are asked online as to which program they use, you'll probably find that most Windows-using genealogists use either Family Tree Maker, RootsMagic, or Legacy Family Tree, while most macOS-using genealogists use either Family Tree Maker, RootsMagic, Reunion, MacFamilyTree, or Heredis. Although genealogy software is not typically expensive, you may want to install free versions for those programs that offer them, to see if you like them well enough to then pay for their additional features.

There is even genealogy software for mobile devices running under Android or iOS/iPadOS, but I find that I need a desktop/laptop computer in order to do real genealogical research. In fact, I have long depended upon having a computer with at least two large displays (and I've recently added a third large display), so that I can look at a genealogical document on one screen while I'm looking at my family tree on the other. Even if you love using your tablet or smartphone and are adept at using them, I strongly suggest that you use a regular desktop or laptop computer for genealogical research. (However, I think that it is fine to have a genealogy app on your mobile device if you are using it only to display your family tree, which can be useful if you are visiting relatives or a cemetery and you want to look something up quickly.)

What exactly does genealogy software let you do? You can use it to:

- record the conclusions you arrived at when you used the Genealogical Proof Standard: the names, dates, locations, and other details about your ancestor's life events, together with copies of the source documents you used and your notes on how you came to your conclusions

- run some data checking against what you typed in, to help catch typos

- search your genealogical information for particular names, when you want to see what you've already found for that person or when you want to add new information

- display ancestors in pedigree charts or family group sheets

- produce simple-to-complex charts to show relationships among multiple ancestors

- produce reports, usually either ancestral reports (showing all the ancestors of someone, typically for yourself) or descendant reports (showing all the descendants of someone, perhaps an immigrant ancestor or one of your more distant ancestors)

- import genealogical information from websites or other programs, or export genealogical information to websites or other programs

While genealogy applications should have all the features listed above, some applications will have additional features, such as fancier charts and reports, or the ability to link the software to online genealogy services so that you can get suggestions (often called "hints") for records that may be about your ancestors.

Organizing files

When I began researching my family in 1992, I ended up accumulating huge amounts of paper. There were handwritten notes, things I printed from genealogy software or from web pages, and documents that I ordered from repositories, such as marriage records. Eventually, I ended up with countless piles of paper. I needed to organize these papers.

If I were starting over today, I would do everything in my power to avoid paper. Paper is easy to lose or accidentally discard. It can be destroyed due to an accident or natural disaster. So, let's look at how to handle paper in the best way.

Paper

- Review each piece of paper to see what it is.
- If it is unique and difficult to obtain a new copy of, such as a document you ordered from a repository, then scan it (we'll talk in the next section about how to handle digital files). Then take the original document and store it using archival-safe sleeves, folders, and boxes. It should then go into a cool, dry, dark place, such as an inside closet. No attics, basements, or garages, if at all possible.
- If it isn't unique, then transcribe it into a digital note, or if it is something that can be easily reprinted, discard it unless you are currently working with that particular piece of paper.
- If you are uncomfortable in working primarily with digital files, then print what you need and file it either in 3-ring binders (one for each family surname) or hanging file folders. This means that you'll need at least one unused shelf for the binders or one unused file cabinet drawer for the file folders, located as close as possible to where you plan to do your online research.
- The suggestions in the next section for digital files can provide you with some ideas as to how to name the sections of your binders or the names on your hanging file folders.

Digital

Today's genealogist is going to end up with a huge number of digital files. Some of these will be the result of scanning paper. Others will be images found on genealogy websites. And others will be files created from genealogy software, such as pedigree charts, family group sheets, other charts, or reports.

You could easily end up with thousands of different files. How do you name them and keep them organized in order to find them as easily as possible?

- Create a high-level folder on your computer named Genealogy. Make sure that this folder is backed up on a regular basis, preferably to a cloud-based backup service. Personally, I use Backblaze for backups. As a result, I sleep at night.
- In your Genealogy folder, create subfolders for each surname that you are researching.
- Also in your Genealogy folder, create two additional subfolders: one called !Inbox, for things that you haven't yet filed in the appropriate subfolder, and one called !Misc, for genealogy-related things that don't fit into one of the surname subfolders.
- In each surname subfolder, create one subfolder for each individual who has that surname. So, in my Smith subfolder, I have one called Smith_George for items pertaining to my father. I use an underscore character to separate the surname and the given name, which avoids confusion with hyphenated names. You can also create !Inbox and !Misc subfolders in each surname folder for things that haven't yet been filed for that surname or that don't pertain to a single individual, such as a group photo.
- Finally, in the subfolder for each individual, put the files that pertain to that person, and name them like this: Surname_Givenname_eventyear_eventtype_documenttype. So, for my father's death certificate, the name of the file would be: Smith_George_1999_death_certificate. This lets all the files sort chronologically, and I can see what each file is at a quick glance, without even having to open it. I can also see what documents I'm missing.
- If you have a file that pertains to more than one person, such as a marriage record or a census record, make a separate digital copy for each individual, and rename each copy to fit the person it pertains to, filing their copy in their own folder.

Browser bookmarks

The ability to keep track of websites that we find especially useful has been part of web browsers for nearly 30 years, and many of us make it a habit to bookmark (or "favorite" in Microsoft Edge) any site that we want to return to quickly and easily. However, we may not be very organized about our bookmarks, resulting in our having hundreds of random bookmarks that make it difficult to find the ones we want to use. So, let's see how best to organize our bookmarks, especially for genealogical research.

First, make use of bookmark folders. Create two folders, one called Genealogy and the other called Genealogy Surnames, and put both folders in your browser's bookmark bar.

In the Genealogy Surnames folder, create a subfolder for each surname as you begin to research it. When you find a website that pertains specifically to your surname of interest, bookmark it and put it in the appropriate surname subfolder.

In the Genealogy folder, put all genealogy-related bookmarks that aren't about specific surnames. Create subfolders for certain categories of resources, such as one called Newspapers.

As you add new bookmarks, edit the name of the bookmark so that the most important identifying word is listed first. This makes it easier for your eye to scan down the list and find the specific bookmark you want.

In any folder, drag the bookmarks that you use most often to the very top of their folder, and rarely used bookmarks to the very bottom.

Chapter 5:
Looking for Previous Research

You've established your genealogical research goal.

You understand the basics of how genealogical research is done.

You've got the tools you need to collect your genealogical research, file it, and organize it.

Your next step is to see what genealogical research has already been done by others. In academic research, this is usually referred to as "the literature review." (By "literature," we don't mean literature in the sense of William Shakespeare or Fyodor Dostoevsky or Toni Morrison, but in the sense of "what has been written about a particular subject." You've probably heard this usage when people talk about "the medical literature" or "the scientific literature.")

Why look at previous research? It's not so that we can say to ourselves, "Well, that's already been done, I don't have to do it again. I can just copy what they've done." Why don't we want to simply copy previous research? Think about the GPS from the previous chapter and ask yourself these questions:

1. What if the original researcher missed some things, either due to carelessness, or because that information simply wasn't known about or easily available when they did the research?
2. What if the original researcher never indicated where they found their information? (If so, how can I even trust it?)
3. What if the original researcher misinterpreted what they found, or did a poor job of putting the information together?
4. What if the original researcher never addressed contradictions in the information? (If so, how did they even come to a conclusion?)
5. What if the original researcher came to a conclusion that isn't really supported by the evidence?

Identifying and Finding Books

When I started my own family research back in the early 1990s, I quickly learned that a few branches of my family (the Boddies and the Eidsons) had already been researched, and the results published in a few family history books.

It was much harder then to find these books, but today, we have tools that can search the catalogs of libraries all over the world. In some cases, the books we are most interested in have been digitized and can be viewed online, either for free or as part of a genealogy subscription service.

Our first step is to identify the books that are relevant to our genealogical research. For each book, we want to find out its exact title, the name of its author(s), and the year it was published. This information can then be used to find copies of the book. We'll use two important library catalogs to identify the books we want: the FamilySearch Catalog and WorldCat.

The FamilySearch Catalog

We'll start by looking at the largest collection of family history books in the world: the FamilySearch Library in downtown Salt Lake City, Utah. There are hundreds of thousands of books in this collection. While there are print books that make up a large part of the collection, there are also books that have been microfilmed. Many of these print and microfilmed books have been digitized and are available for viewing on the FamilySearch website (familysearch.org).

Go to familysearch.org and under Search, choose Catalog. See Figure 5.1 below. (Or you can go directly to familysearch.org/search/catalog, a site that you will want to bookmark in your browser.)

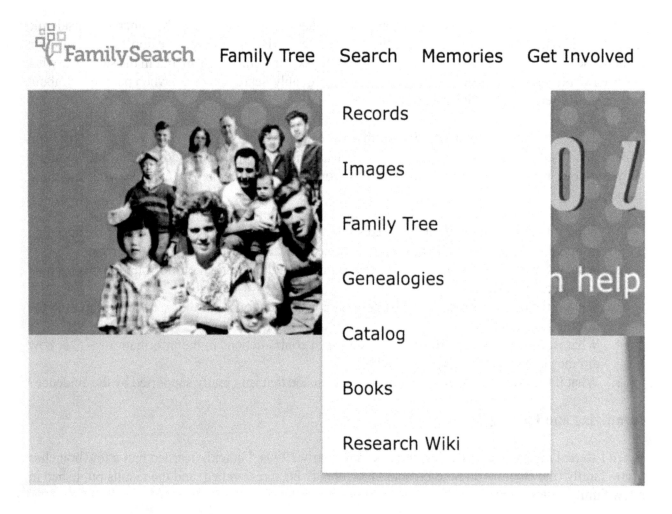

Figure 5.1: FamilySearch Search menu

The FamilySearch Catalog is unlike any other library catalog in the world. While the typical library catalog lets you search by title, author, subject, or keyword, the FamilySearch Catalog also lets you search by place or by surname. At this point, we'll focus on surnames. Click on Surnames, and in the Surnames box, enter a surname that you're researching. Then click the Search button. See Figure 5.2 below.

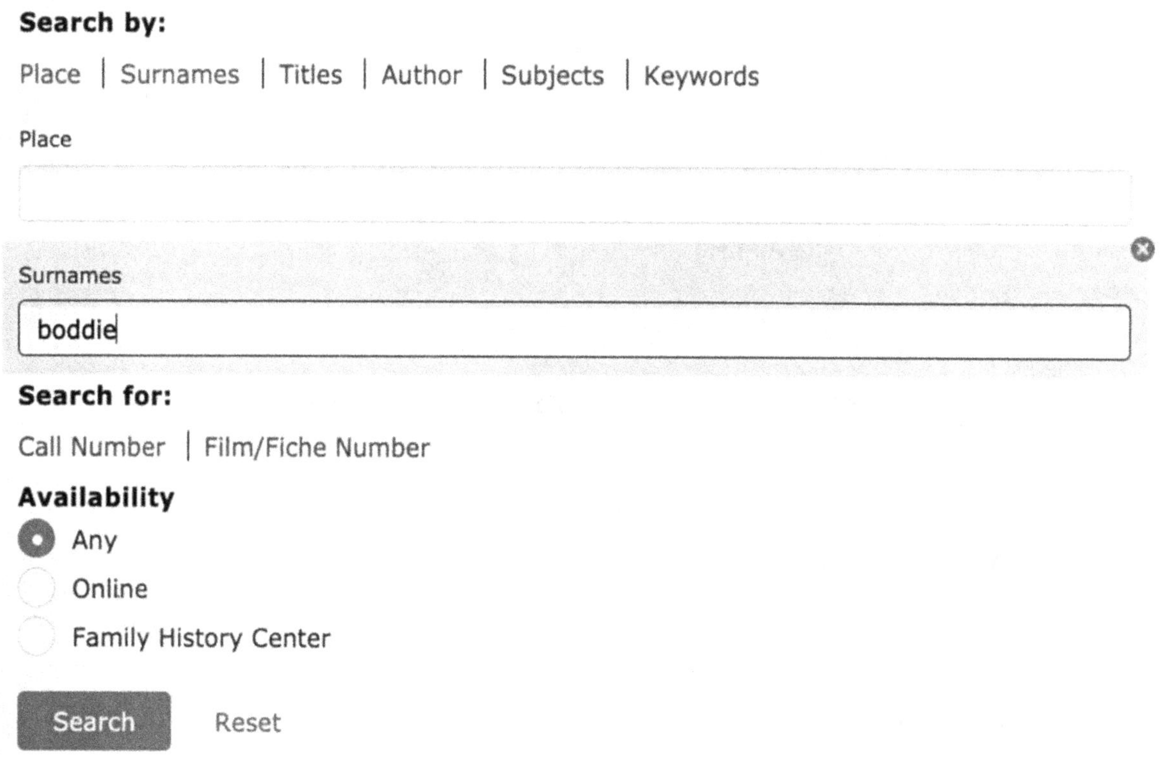

Search by:

Place | Surnames | Titles | Author | Subjects | Keywords

Place

Surnames

boddie

Search for:

Call Number | Film/Fiche Number

Availability

◉ Any

◯ Online

◯ Family History Center

Search   Reset

Figure 5.2: FamilySearch Catalog search screen

Depending upon the surname you entered, you may get "No results found" (typically for a rare surname, such as Weinglass) or thousands of results (typically for a common surname, such as Smith, Martin, or King).

When I search for the surname Boddie, I get 18 results. (See Figure 5.3 on the next page.)

For each book, the FamilySearch Catalog displays:

- the title
- the author(s)

Search Results for FamilySearch Catalog

🖨 PRINT   📑 Catalog Print List (0)

1-18 of 18 results

Alston-Williams-Boddie-Hilliard Society : North Carolina's first family society, instituted and founded by Dr. William M. Mann, Jr., Society and family book, volume I, 1958-1961

   Author: Hilliard, James Byron

   Surname: Boddie

Ancestors of Lucille Irene Hoffman

   Author: Fullerton, Patricia Ann Harris

   Surname: Boddie

Boddie and allied families

   Author: Boddie, John Thomas, b.1864; Boddie, John Bennett, 1880-1965

   Surname: Boddie

Braswell branches

   Author: Williams, Winona Susan Simpson

   Surname: Boddie

Brown, Outlaw and Riggs family history books

   Author: Smith, Mary Eva Riggs

   Surname: Boddie

Freeman family genealogical data, 1570-1973

   Author: Payne, Marguerite E. (Marguerite Eldredge)

   Surname: Boddie

Gillams galore

   Author: Old, Mary A. (Mary Ann Cecilia Gillam), 1945-; Old, Mary A. (Mary Ann Cecilia Gillam), 1945-; Gillams Galore

   Surname: Boddie

Figure 5.3: FamilySearch Catalog search results

I can click the title to see details about the book (see Figures 5.4 and 5.5 on the next pages):

- the year of publication
- the number of pages
- whether or not it has illustrations (ill.)
- the surnames that the book is focused on (this is not going to be a list of every surname that might be mentioned in the book, but will instead be only the most significant ones)

◂ BACK TO SEARCH RESULTS   ⊜ PRINT ▤ Catalog Print List (0)

Boddie and allied families

		Add to Print List
Statement of Responsibility:	by John Thomas Boddie and John Bennett Boddie	
Authors:	Boddie, John Thomas, b.1864 (Main Author)	
	Boddie, John Bennett, 1880-1965 (Added Author)	
Format:	Books/Monographs/Book with Digital Images	
Language:	English	
Publication:	Chicago, Illinois : [s.n.], c1918	
Physical:	[14], 250 p., [16] leaves of plates : ill., col. coats of arms, geneal. tables, ports.	
Subject Class:	929.273 B631	

Notes

To view a digital version of this item click here .

Approximately covers the years 1400-1918.

One leaf of plates is folded.

William Boddy (1634/1635-1717) immigrated from England to Isle of Wight County, Virginia during or before 1661, and married three times (probably once in England). Other early Boddy immigrants are listed. William spelled his surname Boddy, but many records in early Virginia record the surname as Body, Bodye, Bodie, etc. Descendants and relatives lived in Virginia, Kentucky, Indiana, North Carolina, Alabama, Mississippi, Texas and elsewhere. Includes records of various ancestors in England, Scotland and elsewhere to the early 1400s.

Includes index.

Includes bibliographic references.

Includes Battle, Crudup, Drake, Hillard, Kellogg, Lott, Perry, Reynolds, Anderson, Anthony, Arrington, Bennett, Bull, Cannady, Coleman, Dixon, Farrell, Greene, Hinton, Judd, Jones, Lewis, Loomis, Lyman, McNeill, Manning, Marsh, Merrill, Mason, Mildmay, Moore, Mygatt, Peters, Rivers, Rucker, Saunders, Seymour, Stone, Treat, Tunstall, Utter, Watt, Webster, Whiting, Williams, Winston, Young, Yancey, Yandell and related families.

Also available on microfilm and digital images.

View this catalog record in WorldCat for other possible copy locations ⊕

Figure 5.4: Book publication details

Subjects
Surname Subjects

Boddie	Bull	Marsh	Tunstall
Body	Cannady	Merrill	Utter
Bodye	Coleman	Mason	Watt
Bodie	Dixon	Mildmay	Webster
Battle	Drake	Moore	Whiting
Crudup	Farrell	Mygatt	Williams
Hillard	Greene	Peters	Winston
Kellogg	Hinton	Reynolds	Young
Lott	Judd	Rivers	Yancey
Perry	Jones	Rucker	Yandell
Anderson	Lewis	Saunders	McNeill
Anthony	Loomis	Seymour	
Arrington	Lyman	Stone	
Bennett	Manning	Treat	

Location

Family History Library	⌄

Copies

Call Number	Location	Collection/Shelf	Availability
929.273 B631b	Family History Library	Family History Off-site Storage	Off-site Storage

Film/Digital Notes

Note	Location	Collection/Shelf	Film	Image Group Number (DGS)	Format
Also on microfilm. Salt Lake City : Filmed by the Genealogical Society of Utah, 1986. on 1 microfilm reel ; 35 mm.	Family History Library	United States & Canada 2nd Floor Film	1321116 Item 1	7968769	🎞

Figure 5.5: Surnames and availability of the book

If the book has been digitized, I can click a link to view the digital copy. If FamilySearch has digitized a book, any print copy is no longer needed and is normally moved to an off-site storage location in order to free up physical library space.

For relatively rare surnames, such as Boddie, I can be reasonably certain that all of the listed books will be relevant to my own family. But if I were looking at a more common surname, I would likely find large numbers of books that are about people with the same surname, but who are not related to my family (or at least, where I could see no evidence that they are). I can use the Place search box to limit my search to locations that I know to be associated with my family. As it is with any kind of search for information, the tricky part is trying to narrow it down to only those items that are relevant without accidentally leaving out relevant results. This is a skill that you'll develop the more searches that you do.

For each relevant book that has been digitized, bookmark the link to the digital copy in your bookmark folder for that surname. For each relevant book that has *not* been digitized, bookmark the FamilySearch Catalog entry instead.

Although FamilySearch does have the largest number of family history books in any one library, it does not have every family history book that has ever been published. So, we'll need to look to at least one other catalog to see if we've missed any: WorldCat.

WorldCat

All public and academic (university and college) libraries have their own library catalogs to identify the books in their collections, and many of them keep a copy of their catalog records in the same union catalog. (A *union catalog* is a catalog that combines the catalogs from a number of different libraries, such as for a country or for a U.S. state.) The largest online union catalog is WorldCat, produced and maintained by OCLC, Inc., and containing the holdings of thousands of libraries around the world.

You can search WorldCat for genealogy books at worldcat.org. I recommend clicking its "Advanced search" link to give you some additional search options. See Figure 5.6 below.

Figure 5:6: WorldCat home page

Because WorldCat, unlike the FamilySearch Catalog, is not a catalog dedicated to genealogy, WorldCat doesn't provide us with a surname search option. Instead, we have to use "Subject" searching instead, where the subject is the surname followed by the word "family." Follow these steps (and see Figure 5.7 below):

- Change the first dropdown menu from *Keyword:* to *Subject:*
- In the field, enter the surname of interest immediately followed by the word "family"
- Under Format, choose *Book*
- Click the Search button

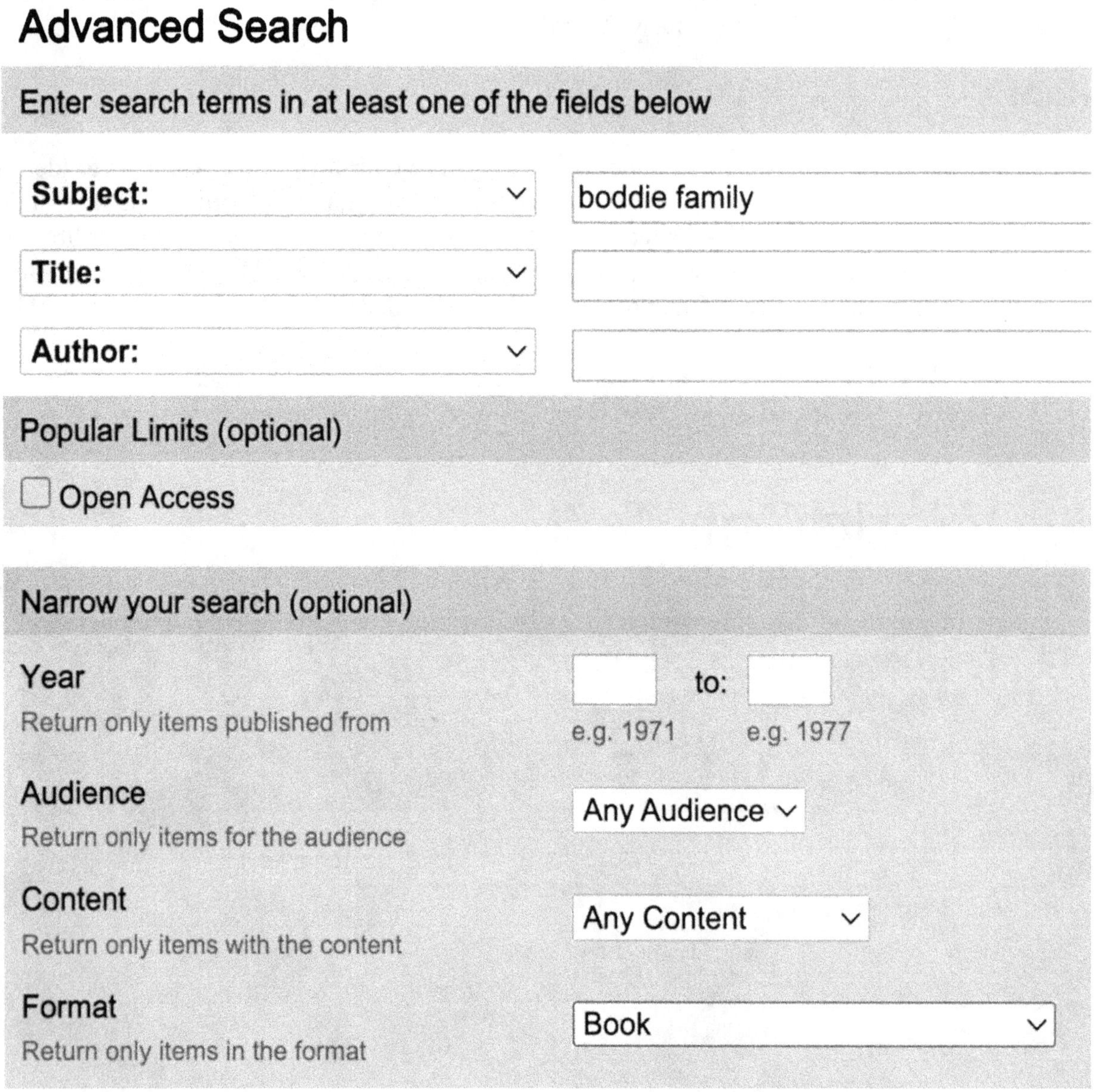

Advanced Search

Enter search terms in at least one of the fields below

| **Subject:** ⌄ | boddie family |

| **Title:** ⌄ | |

| **Author:** ⌄ | |

Popular Limits (optional)

☐ Open Access

Narrow your search (optional)

Year
Return only items published from

    to:
e.g. 1971   e.g. 1977

Audience
Return only items for the audience

Any Audience ⌄

Content
Return only items with the content

Any Content ⌄

Format
Return only items in the format

Book ⌄

Figure 5.7: WorldCat Advanced Search

When I search for the surname Boddie, I get 13 results. See Figure 5.8 below. For each book, WorldCat displays:

- the title
- the author(s)
- the format of the book (such as digital or print)
- the name of the publisher and the publisher's location
- the year of publication

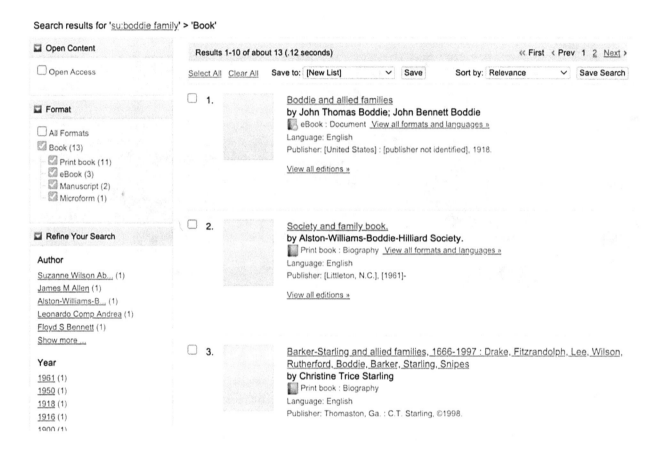

Figure 5.8: WorldCat search results

For each book you find, bookmark its WorldCat entry.

In a later section of this chapter, I'll talk about how you can use the information provided by WorldCat to find a print copy of the book.

Why search multiple catalogs? Let's compare my search in WorldCat, which resulted in 13 books, with my previous search in the FamilySearch Catalog, which resulted in 18 books. Six of the same books appeared in both lists. But each of the two catalogs had items that the other catalog didn't have. Searching both catalogs helps us locate as many relevant books as possible.

Digital books

Many thousands of family history books have been digitized and made available online, either for free (such as the FamilySearch Digital Library shown below in Figure 5.9) or as part of a subscription service (such as MyHeritage shown on the following pages in Figures 5.10 and 5.11). This means that you can search across multiple books looking for references to your ancestors.

FamilySearch Digital Library (familysearch.org/library/books)

Figure 5.9: FamilySearch Digital Library home screen

The FamilySearch Digital Library contains a collection of digitized books and other genealogical materials. Different books will have different *Access Levels* (the following lists the most common):

- Public (The book is no longer under copyright protection, so it is in the public domain, and can be accessed from anywhere, including from your home.)
- Full Permission (The book is still under copyright protection, but the copyright owner has given permission for the book to be viewed online from any location, as well as permission for downloading and printing.)
- Limited Permission (The book is still under copyright protection, but the copyright owner has given permission for the book to be viewed online from any location; however, permission has not been given for downloading or printing.)
- Protected (The book is still under copyright protection, and the copyright owner has not given permission for the book to be viewed online.)

MyHeritage

The subscription site MyHeritage, as part of its Books & Publications collections, provides access to two large collections pointing us to books and other publications that may refer to our ancestors: the Historical Books – Index of Authors and People Mentioned, 1811-2003; and the Compilation of Published Sources

The Historical Books collection indexes more than 3 million books. A link may be provided to an online repository where the actual image can be viewed. If not, the record will at least tell you the title of the book, its year of publication, and who published it, in order to find the book in other ways.

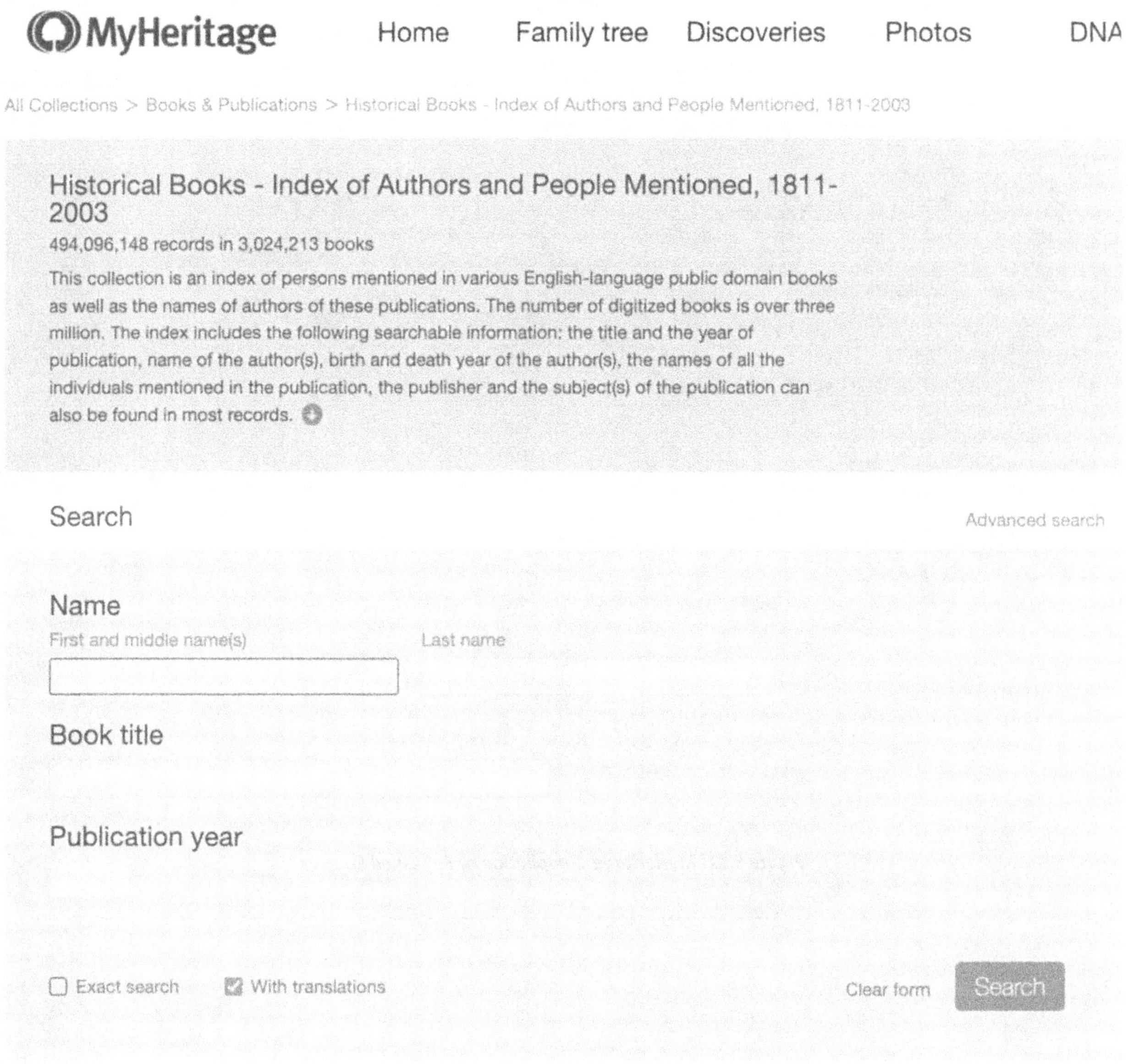

Figure 5.10: MyHeritage Historical Books

The Compilation of Published Sources has the actual images for nearly 500,000 published sources.

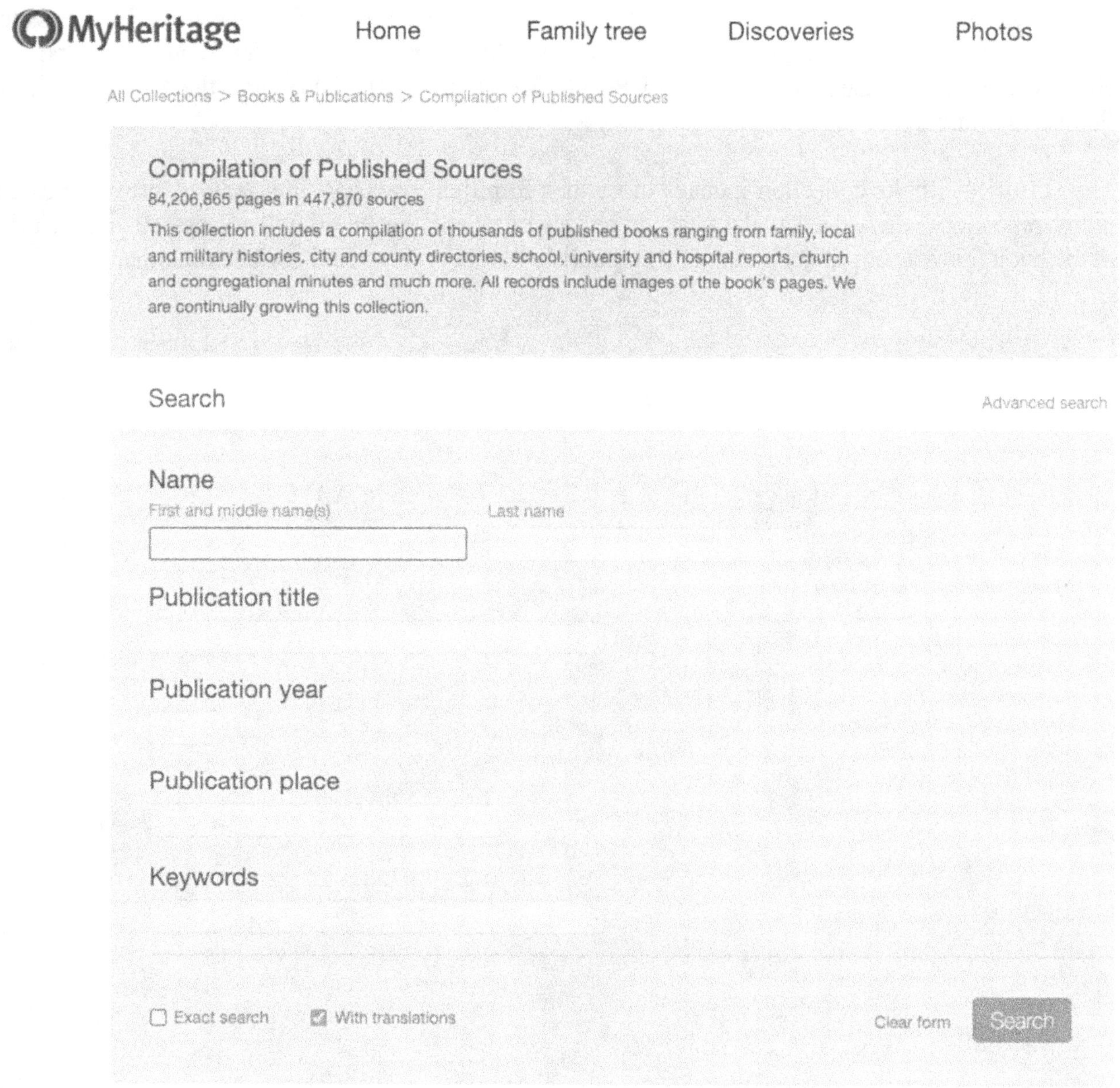

Figure 5.11: MyHeritage Compilation of Published Sources

Print books

If you have identified a family history book that discusses some part of your family, but the book is not available for you to read online, you may be able to obtain a print copy.

In WorldCat, you can click a book's title to see more details about the book. See Figure 5.12 below. The most important information that you can now discover is a list of the libraries that have a copy of the book ("Find a copy in the library"). By entering your zip code ("Enter your location:"), you can be shown a list of all libraries holding the book, from nearest to farthest. Clicking the name of the library will take you to that library's website, which will provide you with its location, hours of operation, and contact information in case you want to communicate with the library. Some libraries will be willing to scan pages from the book's index, and then you can use that information to request scans of specific pages that may be about your family.

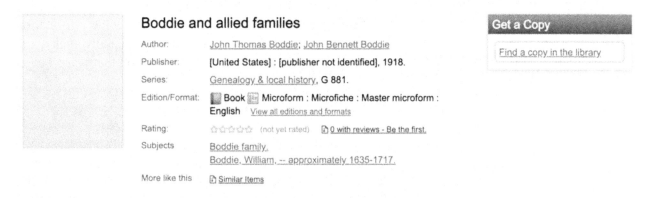

Figure 5.12: WorldCat's list of libraries holding a particular book

Another option is to see if the book is available for purchase, either as out-of-print or as a used copy. There are three websites to use to find out-of-print or used books (see Figures 5.13, 5.14, and 5.15):

- AddALL (used.addall.com)
- BookFinder (bookfinder.com)
- viaLibri (vialibri.net)

These sites obtain information provided by over 100,000 booksellers from around the world. Instead of your having to visit hundreds of different websites, these three megasites make it possible to search among millions of books. While there is very likely to be a lot of overlap among the three sites, it's worth the time to do a quick search on all of them to maximize your chances of locating an out-of-print or used copy of a family history book.

Generally, these sites list the least expensive copies first. These cheaper copies may be slightly damaged or may have notes handwritten into the books. However, if all you need is the information in the book, this shouldn't be much of a factor in your decision. If you're especially lucky, the handwritten notes in a family history book may even include additional information that wasn't even part of the original book.

Figure 5:13 AddALL search results

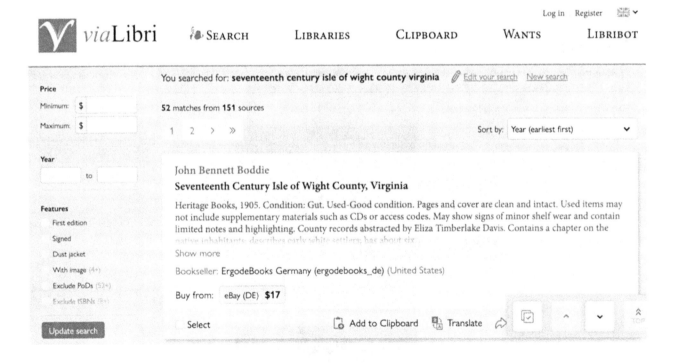

Figure 5.14: BookFinder.com search results

Figure 5.15: viaLibri search results

Periodicals (journals, magazines, and newsletters)

Your genealogical literature review should not be limited to books. Many genealogists over the past 200-plus years have written about families in genealogical and historical periodicals instead of in books. By periodicals, I mean journals, magazines, and newsletters. Most of these have been published by genealogical or historical societies, while others have been published by family associations.

Finding out if your own family has been written about in some periodical would take a lot of effort, if it were not for the great work done by the Genealogy Center of the Allen County Public Library (ACPL) in Fort Wayne, Indiana. The ACPL Genealogy Center has made it their mission to obtain copies of as many genealogical periodical issues as they could, and then index the contents of those issues by surname, location, and type of record. (They also index how-to articles.) The result is the *Periodical Source Index (PERSI)*, a database of more than 3 million entries, updated quarterly (see Figure 5.16 below). PERSI is available online at https://genealogycenter.info/persi

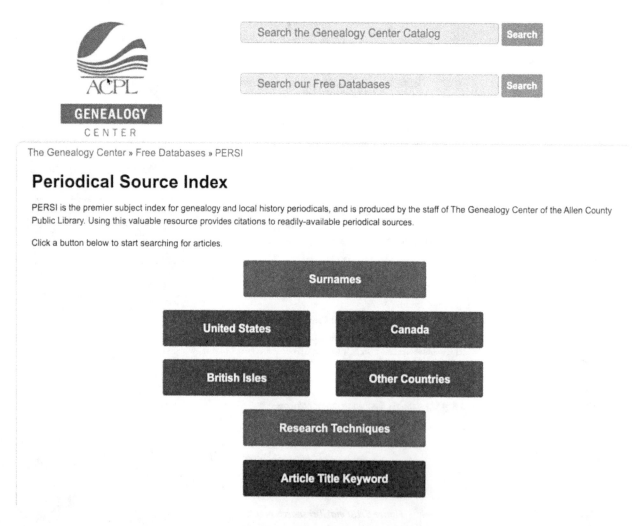

Figure 5.16: Periodical Source Index home page

PERSI provides these details:

- the name of the publisher (usually a genealogical or historical society) and their address
- the volume number
- the month or season of publication
- the issue number
- the 4-character PERSI code for that periodical

You have several options to obtain a copy of the article:

- contact your local library to see if they can obtain a copy of the article using interlibrary loan (ILL)
- search WorldCat for the name of the periodical to find out what libraries have copies, and contact them directly to see if they would scan the article you need and send it to you
- send an order form (there is a small fee) to the Allen County Public Library Foundation, requesting the articles that you need. The form is available at this link: https://acpl-cms.wise.oclc.org/images/Documents/Gendocs/Forms/articlerequest.pdf

Archival material (manuscripts)

Many people who do genealogical research never get to the point of publishing their work in a book or in a periodical article. Instead, they may simply collect their research results as part of a set of their personal papers. In some cases, these papers are donated to an archival repository, often part of an academic (university or college) library, public library, or historical society. To find out if you have ancestors mentioned in *archival material* (also referred to as *manuscripts*), you can use WorldCat. See Figures 5.17 through 5.20 on the next several pages.

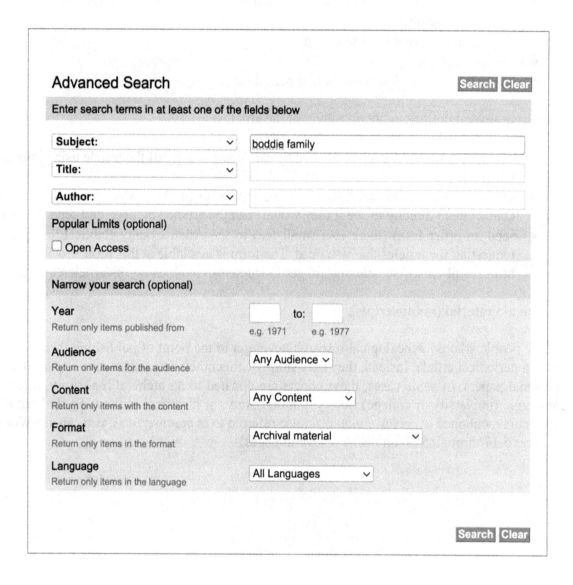

Figure 5.17: WorldCat search for archival material about a family (surname)

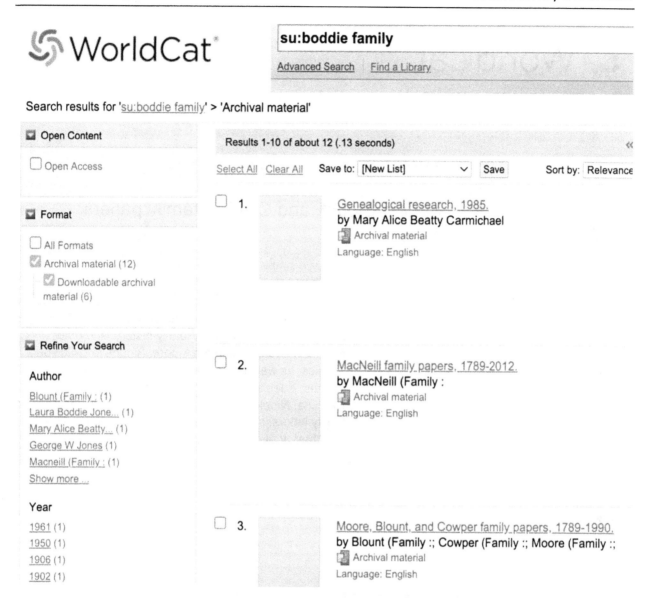

Figure 5.18: WorldCat archival material search results

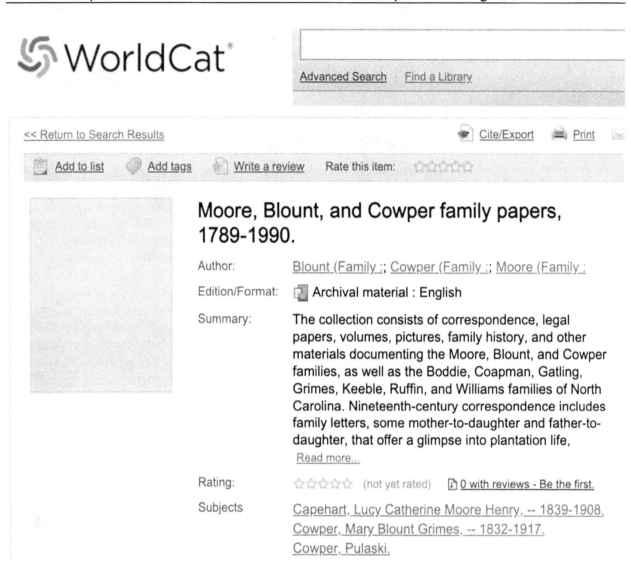

Figure 5.19: WorldCat entry for a particular collection of archival material (summary)

Figure 5.20: WorldCat entry for a particular collection of archival material (details)

WorldCat will give you a brief description of the archival material and provide you with a link to the library that has it. The link may take you directly to the entry in the library's catalog for that specific collection of archival material. See Figure 5.21 below and 5.22 on the next page.

Figure 5.21: WorldCat link to archival material repository

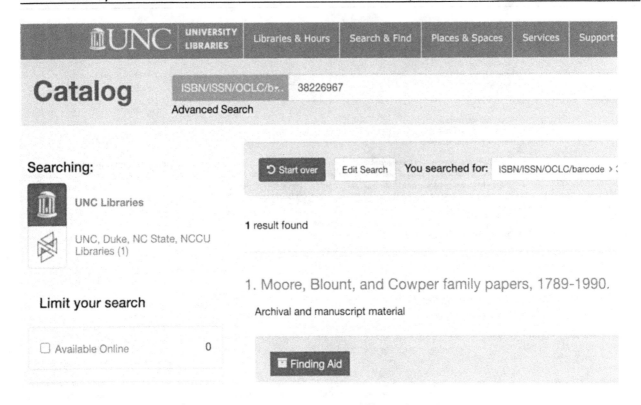

Figure 5.22: University of North Carolina Libraries catalog entry for collection of archival material

The next thing to look for is a link to a *finding aid*. A finding aid is a detailed description of what is in the collection. It may tell you:

- how large the collection is
- an abstract (summary) of what is in the collection
- who created the collection
- the language of the collection
- whether or not there are any restrictions on accessing or using the collection
- who holds the copyright (if copyright is still in effect)
- how to cite the collection
- how the collection was acquired
- what library subjects the collection is catalogued under
- additional details about the scope and content of the collection

See Figures 5.23 and 5.24 on the next page for an example of a finding aid.

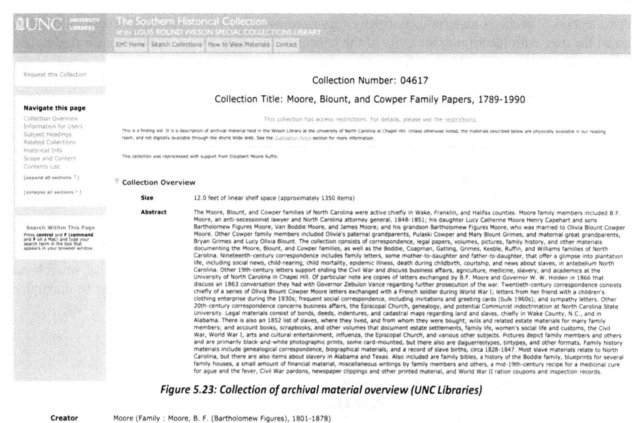

Figure 5.23: Collection of archival material overview (UNC Libraries)

Creator	Moore (Family : Moore, B. F. (Bartholomew Figures), 1801-1878)
	Blount (Family : Blount, John Gray, 1752-1833)
	Cowper (Family : Cowper, Pulaski)
Language	English

Back to Top

▼ Information For Users

Restrictions to Access

This collection contains additional materials that are not available for immediate or same day access. Please contact Research and Instructional Service staff at wilsonlibrary@unc.edu to discuss options for consulting these materials.

Restrictions to Use

No usage restrictions.

Copyright Notice

Copyright is retained by the authors of items in these papers, or their descendants, as stipulated by United States copyright law.

Preferred Citation

[Identification of item], in the Moore, Blount, and Cowper Family Papers #4617, Southern Historical Collection, The Wilson Library, University of North Carolina at Chapel Hill.

Acquisitions Information

Received from Olivia Blount Cowper Moore of Raleigh, N.C., in June 1992 (Acc. 92077) and from her estate in November 1992 (Acc. 92166).

Sensitive Materials Statement

Manuscript collections and archival records may contain materials with sensitive or confidential information that is protected under federal or state right to privacy laws and regulations, the North Carolina Public Records Act (N.C.G.S. § 132 1 et seq.), and Article 7 of the North Carolina State Personnel Act (Privacy of State Employee Personnel Records, N.C.G.S. § 126-22 et seq.). Researchers are advised that the disclosure of certain information pertaining to identifiable living individuals represented in this collection without the consent of those individuals may have legal ramifications (e.g., a cause of action under common law for invasion of privacy may arise if facts concerning an individual's private life are published that would be deemed highly offensive to a reasonable person) for which the University of North Carolina at Chapel Hill assumes no responsibility.

Figure 5.24: Collection of archival material information for users (UNC Libraries)

A collection of archival material is normally organized by series (or boxes) and folders. In order to assist the user with identifying the parts of the collection that they would like to see, the finding aid will give details as to what is in each series/box and in each folder.

At this point, you have two options:

1. contact the library to see if they would scan a few specific items from the collection to send to you
2. visit the library to see the collection for yourself (or arrange for a relative or friend to visit the library on your behalf)

Visiting libraries and archives

Before you hop in a car or a plane to visit a repository that might have a book, periodical, or archival material about your family, there are several things that you should do first in order to maximize success:

Visit the repository's website to learn:

- The exact information needed to specifically identify the item you want
  - for a book, its title, author, and location within the library (usually a call number)
  - for a periodical article, the title of the periodical, the title of the article, its date of publication, and its location within the library
  - for archival material, the name of the collection and the specific series/box and folder you need
- Whether or not the material you are interested in is under any access restrictions
- Whether or not the repository requires appointments
- The repository's dates and hours of operations, including any planned closures for holidays or renovations. Note that a public library's genealogy collection or an academic library's special collections may have more restricted dates/hours than the library as a whole.
- Directions to the facility including suggestions for available parking
- The repository's policies regarding what you are allowed to bring into the research rooms
- Contact information for the repository: names (when available), email addresses, and phone numbers

Reach out to the repository to:

1. Verify that the facility will be open on the date/time you plan to visit
2. Make appointments if needed
3. Request items to be pulled from the archive so that they will be immediately available to you on the date/time you visit
4. Ask if there is a particular librarian or archivist that you could talk to about your research who might be especially familiar with what their facility might have for your family

Chapter 6:
DNA Testing

Now that you've had the chance to look for any genealogical research that has already been done about your family, you must be eager to get going with your own research. But there is one last thing that is worth starting before you start with traditional research: DNA testing.

What's the hurry? Well, the traditional genealogical records found in libraries, archives, courthouses, cemeteries, and other physical locations are very likely to be there waiting for you whenever you get around to using them. Only a very small percentage of physical records are lost due to natural disaster or human negligence, and every day, more and more physical records are digitized and put online so that we don't even have to visit a physical repository to see them.

The problem is our living relatives won't be around forever. Because we never know when we might lose them, we should be sure not only to collect the stories that they remember about the family, but also to think about how we should use DNA testing for genealogical purposes while we are still able to obtain a DNA sample from them.

So, let's look at the very basics of DNA testing and how it can help our research.

What is DNA, and why is it useful for genealogical research?

DNA is a complex chemical molecule that determines the physical structure of living things. In humans, DNA is copied and passed down from both biological parents to their children.

All humans share with each other a great deal of the same DNA (the part that makes us human as opposed to some other living species). But there is always a small portion of our DNA that makes each of us unique individuals, with the exception of identical twins.

Even though we each have unique DNA, we share a lot of that DNA with our closest relatives. The closer the relative, the more DNA we share with them. This means that we can use DNA testing to help with determining likely relationships between two people. In some cases, DNA testing can be used to rule out relationships.

What are the different types?

All living things can be divided into two groups based on the structure of their cells: those that have cells with a *nucleus* surrounded by a nuclear envelope (also called a nuclear membrane), and those without.

Those living things *without* an envelope-enclosed nucleus include bacteria and some other microorganisms. Those living things *with* an envelope-enclosed nucleus include all fungi, plants, and animals (such as humans). For those living things, each cell contains both a nucleus and a number of *organelles* (subunits outside the nucleus that provide specific biological functions). One type of organelle is *mitochondria*, which provide energy to the cells.

So, the two major types of DNA found in all humans are:

- Mitochondrial DNA (mtDNA)
- Nuclear DNA

Nuclear DNA can be further subdivided into two types:

- autosomal DNA (atDNA)
- sex chromosomes (also known as allosomal DNA)

The human sex chromosomes consist of two types:

- X chromosomes (X-DNA)
- Y chromosomes (Y-DNA)

We'll look at each of those types and learn how they can help us in our genealogical research. But before we discuss mtDNA and Y-DNA, we need to understand an additional concept: *mutation*.

Mutation

DNA is a molecule that has its own mechanisms for making copies of itself. But biological copying processes are not perfect. There can be changes to the DNA during the process, and even additions or deletions of small bits of DNA. These genetic changes are known as *mutations*. In a few cases, mutations can result in genetic diseases. In most cases, mutations are harmless.

Both mtDNA and Y-DNA are normally copied exactly from generation to generation, but there can be mutations. We'll discuss those mutations in the next two sections.

Mitochondrial DNA (mtDNA)

Mitochondrial DNA is the DNA found in mitochondria (the singular is *mitochondrion*). There are tens of trillions of cells in the human body, and each of those cells has some mitochondria. Depending on the type of human cell, the cell could have only a few mitochondria, or it could have thousands. Mitochondria have their own DNA that is separate from the cell's nuclear DNA. Because the human body has so many mitochondria, mtDNA is often the easiest kind of DNA to be obtained from human remains, even from people who were alive tens of thousands of years ago.

See Figure 6.1 on the next page for a diagram of where mitochondria can be found in the human cell, and what mtDNA looks like.

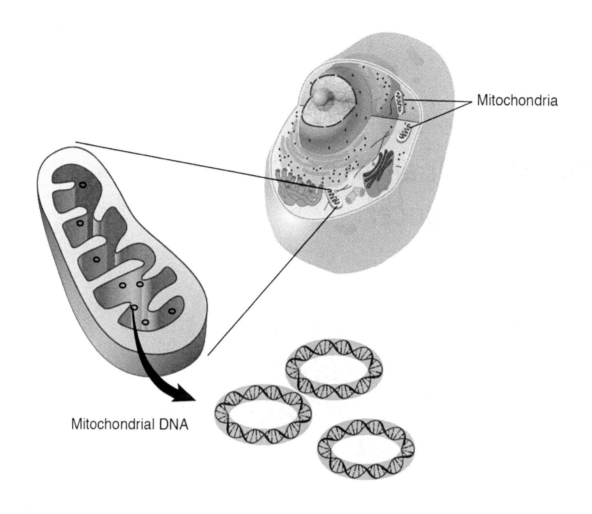

Mitochondria

Mitochondrial DNA

Figure 6.1: Mitochondrial DNA (Source: National Human Genome Research Institute).

When human conception occurs, and the egg cell and sperm cell combine into a fertilized egg, the mitochondria from the sperm cell is discarded (with very rare exceptions that we don't need to worry about). This means that the child resulting from this process will have a copy of only its mother's mtDNA, and no copy of its father's mtDNA.

Because mtDNA is inherited by all people only from their mothers, mtDNA testing can help us only with genealogical research questions relating to those people in our direct *matrilineal* line. If we test our own mtDNA, the results can't help us with knowing anything about our father's family, or our maternal grandfather's family, or any other person who isn't in the line of women from our mothers stretching back through the generations of women (daughter to mother).

See Figure 6.2 on the next page for an illustration of the inheritance pattern of mitochondrial DNA.

71

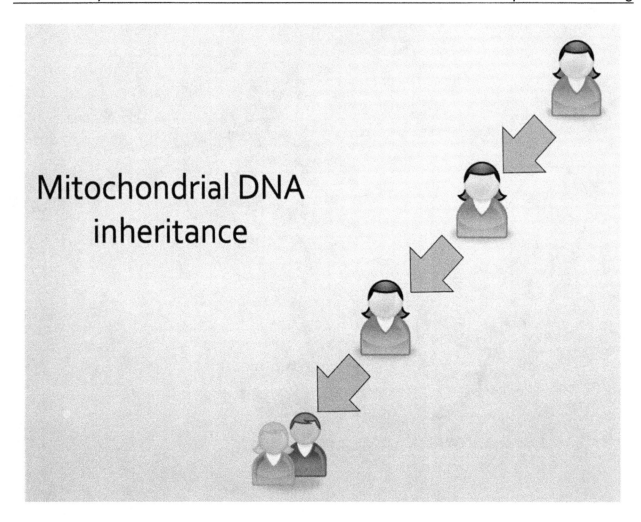

Figure 6.2: Mitochondrial DNA inheritance

mtDNA mutates very slowly over the generations. This means that you may have the exact same mtDNA as your matrilineal ancestor from hundreds of years ago. So will her other matrilineal descendants. As a result, even if you and another person match perfectly on your mtDNA, your common ancestor might be hundreds of years in the past. This means that mtDNA testing isn't generally worth doing just to try to establish who your common ancestor was but is more useful if you are trying to rule out having a particular common ancestor.

The only company doing mtDNA testing useful for genealogical purposes is FamilyTreeDNA (FTDNA). Their mtFULL Sequence (sometimes called Full Mitochondrial Sequence, abbreviated as FMS) tests the entire mitochondrial genome.

See Figure 6.3 on the next page for an example of the matching results from a mitochondrial DNA test taken with FTDNA.

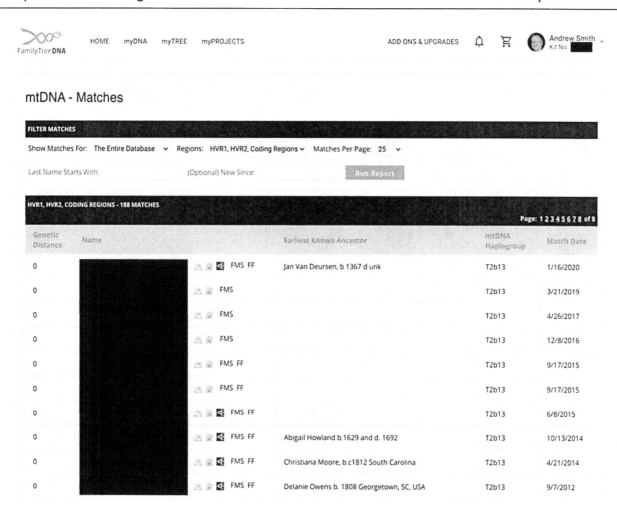

Figure 6.3: FamilyTreeDNA mtDNA match results

Y-DNA

Y-DNA is one of the sex chromosomes found in the nuclear DNA. As a general rule, humans with one X-chromosome and one Y-chromosome are genetically male, while humans with two X-chromosomes are genetically female. (Certainly, there are exceptions such as intersexed individuals, and we are not talking about gender identification. Those topics are beyond the scope of this book.)

Because only males have Y-DNA, this means that they must have inherited it from their fathers. And those fathers inherited it from *their* fathers. This means that Y-DNA is inherited along only the *patrilineal* line. See Figure 6.4 on the next page for an illustration of the inheritance pattern of Y-DNA.

As it happens, in most European cultures (and the cultures of their descendants in other continents), children are most frequently given the surname of their father. This means that Y-DNA tends to be passed down along with the surname, from father to son. I can refer to my own Y-DNA as the "Smith Y-DNA" (keeping in mind that there will be many different Smith Y-chromosomes, since not all Smiths are related). I have the same Y-DNA as my father, my paternal grandfather, his father, and so on, back to the immigrant Smith ancestor and beyond.

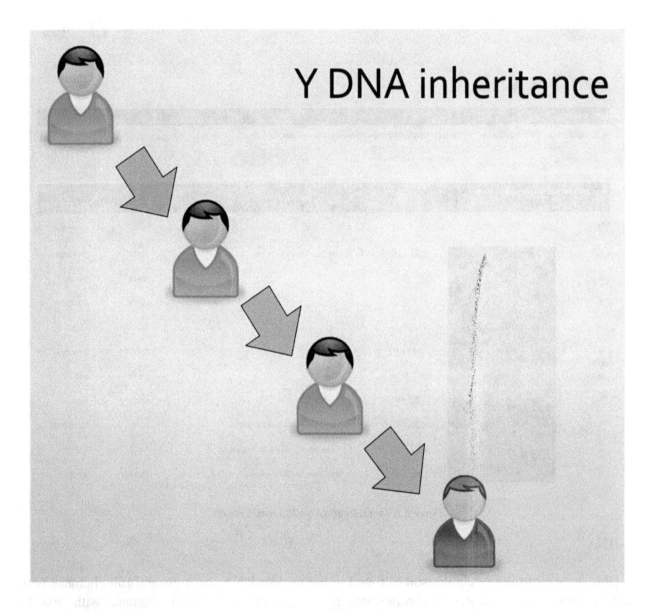

Figure 6.4: Y-DNA inheritance

Y-DNA does mutate, so it is certainly possible for a father and a son to have very slightly different Y-DNA. It is far more common for them to have the exact same Y-DNA. I would expect to have the exact same Y-DNA as my brother, my male Smith first cousins, my male Smith second cousins, and so on, although the more distant the Smith cousin, the higher the chance that our Y-DNA will not match perfectly.

Y-DNA testing can be used to see if two males with the same surname are related, and if a lot of males with the same surname are related, Y-DNA testing can help estimate which ones are more likely to be more closely related than the others. So, Y-DNA testing can be useful when doing genealogical research involving tracing surnames back in time.

As with mtDNA, the only company doing Y-DNA testing useful for genealogical purposes is FamilyTreeDNA. It is generally recommended to start with a Y-37 test, and then that test can be upgraded later to a more detailed test. See Figure 6.5 for an example of the results of an FTDNA Y-DNA test.

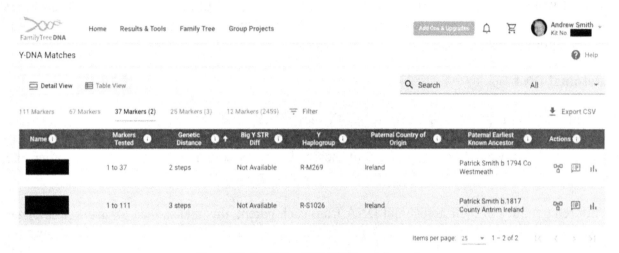

Figure 6.5: FamilyTreeDNA Y-DNA match results

If you have male relatives who are the last surviving males with their surname, it can be important to have their Y-DNA tested while they are still alive. FTDNA will store their sample after testing so that it can be used for additional DNA tests, even if the test taker has since passed away.

Genetic Recombination (Genetic Reshuffling)

Before we discuss autosomal DNA and X-DNA, we need to cover one last concept: *genetic recombination* (also known as *genetic reshuffling*). Humans typically have 22 pairs of autosomal chromosomes and one pair of sex chromosomes. In each pair, one of those chromosomes came from the mother and the other from the father. In other words, the egg cell originally had 23 chromosomes, as did the sperm cell, so the fertilized egg ended up with 23 pairs.

But where did the 23 chromosomes in the egg cell and the 23 chromosomes in the sperm cell come from? If the mother herself had 23 pairs of chromosomes, how did she produce 23 unpaired chromosomes for the egg cell? (Same question regarding the father and the sperm cell.)

The answer is that when the egg cells and sperm cells are produced, their chromosomes are *combinations* of the ones that the parent has. So, while the mother has a pair of Chromosome 1 (the longest chromosome), her egg cells have a single Chromosome 1 that is a combination of the original pair. And like the shuffling of two decks of 52 cards each to produce a single deck of 52 cards (imagine that 52 of the cards are discarded in the shuffled deck), the result will be different every time. Each egg cell will have a different combination of the pair of Chromosome 1, and the other autosomal pairs. The same happens with the sperm cell.

This explains why siblings are not identical twins. They each receive a different combination (shuffling) of each pair of their parents' chromosomes. (Real identical twins come from the same single fertilized egg, so they do have the exact same DNA.)

Note that while everything just described about recombination applies to the 22 pairs of *autosomal* chromosomes, there are exceptions regarding the *sex* chromosomes, discussed in the later section about X chromosomes.

Autosomal DNA

As mentioned in the previous section on genetic recombination, autosomal DNA is nuclear DNA that is passed from parent to child as a mixture of each of the parents' pairs. Children, then, have 50% of their mother's autosomal DNA and 50% of their father's autosomal DNA, and siblings (other than identical twins) have their own unique mixture from each parent.

If children get 50% of their autosomal DNA from each parent, this means that, *on average*, they get 25% of their autosomal DNA from each grandparent. But this is an average, since a parent does not have to pass to their own children exactly half of the DNA from each of their own parents. They might pass down more from one parent than the other. So, a child could have a little more DNA from their paternal grandfather and a little less from their paternal grandmother, or vice versa. The same for their maternal grandparents.

This continues for each generation. We get, *on average*, 12.5% of our DNA from each great-grandparent, 6.25% from each great-great-grandparent, and so on. But because we could get less or more from each ancestor prior to our parents, we will eventually reach a point enough generations back where one or more of our ancestors will not have given us any DNA at all.

If we didn't get any DNA from one of our ancestors, does this mean that we aren't descended from them? No. We have two family trees: a *genealogical* tree and a *genetic* tree. The genealogical tree has all the people we are descended from. The genetic tree is a subset of that tree. It has only all the people we inherited DNA from.

While we do share a lot of DNA with our siblings, we also share some DNA with all our first cousins and all our second cousins. Once we get to relatives more distant than second cousins, we run into the situation where we might not share any DNA with them, because the same DNA was not passed down along both ancestral lines from our common ancestor to each of us. You'll match most, but not all, of your third cousins, and some, but not most, of your fourth cousins, and even fewer of your fifth and sixth cousins and beyond. However, if you have siblings, it's entirely possible that your sibling will match a third cousin (or more distant) that you don't, or vice versa. This means that it is very helpful to your genealogical research to get all of your siblings to do DNA testing. (And if possible, the same for your first cousins and second cousins.)

All of the major DNA testing companies offer autosomal DNA tests. AncestryDNA and 23andMe are the most popular, which means that their databases have the largest number of people who have tested. If you can test with only one, start with AncestryDNA, but if you can afford it, test with both. You can also test with the other major companies: MyHeritage, FamilyTreeDNA, and Living DNA. (FamilyTreeDNA calls their autosomal DNA test "Family Finder".) Or you can download your autosomal DNA data from any of the companies and upload it to MyHeritage, FamilyTreeDNA, and Living DNA. Figures 6.6 through 6.10 at the end of this chapter illustrate the results of autosomal DNA testing with the major DNA testing companies.

Each of the major companies that does DNA testing provides you with at least two types of results: ethnicity estimates and relative matching.

Ethnicity estimates are certainly interesting and informative, but because they are just that, estimates, they may point to ethnic backgrounds that you don't actually have. Whatever ethnicity results you get, use them as ideas of where unknown ancestors might have come from, but don't make any assumptions that they are 100% correct.

From a genealogical perspective, relative matching is the most useful thing that you can get from taking an autosomal DNA test. First, you can expect to match known relatives who may also have tested with the same company. Certainly, you'll match your parents, grandparents, siblings, aunts, uncles, nieces, nephews, first cousins, and second cousins, and you can expect to match many of your more distant cousins.

Because your parents, aunts, uncles, and cousins are on specific sides of your family, you can use their tests to help you figure out how you might be related to some unknown match. For instance, an unknown match (who matches you) might also match your mother, but not your father. So, you could use that information to determine that the unknown match is related to you on your mother's side.

Try to get as many of your second cousins to test as possible, because you'll be able to use their match lists to see which one matches one of your unknown matches. You've narrowed your relationship to the unknown match to the descendants of the great-grandparents you share with that second cousin.

X-DNA

In fathers, their two sex chromosomes cannot recombine (since one is an X and the other is a Y), so their sperm cells just contain either a copy of the X-chromosome that they got from their own mother (which will result in a daughter) or the Y-chromosome that they got from their own father (which will result in a son).

In mothers, their two sex chromosomes, both being an X-chromosome, *can* recombine with each other, and this is what usually happens (approximately 86% of the time). But when a mother produces an egg cell, there is also a 7% chance that she simply passes along a copy of the X-chromosome that she got from her own mother, and a 7% chance that she simply passes along a copy of the X-chromosome that she got from her own father. Because of this, X-DNA can be passed down through more generations, on average, than autosomal DNA can.

DNA testing companies do not offer separate X-DNA tests. Instead, they test X-DNA as part of testing autosomal DNA.

The ethics of DNA testing

Because 50% of autosomal DNA is lost in each new generation, it's a good idea to get your oldest relatives (those from the earliest generations) to do DNA testing while they are still alive and able to do so. And the more siblings, first cousins, and second cousins you can get to test, the easier it will be for you to figure out where any unknown DNA matches fit into your family.

However, anyone who does DNA testing needs to understand what can happen. In particular, family secrets can be revealed. A test taker may learn that one or both of their parents are not their biological parents, or that one of their grandparents was not their biological grandparent.

You could be contacted by someone who was adopted or who had an unknown father and who has matched you or one of your close relatives whose DNA test you are managing. If one of your oldest female relatives gave up a child in secret many decades ago, and she does a DNA test today, she may not realize that her secret may come to light. Or if one of your male relatives secretly fathered a child (whether knowingly or unknowingly), that secret might be revealed.

The point is that you need to make certain that anyone who does a DNA test for you (yourself included) understands what might happen. Don't engage in DNA testing if you're not sure that you are willing to handle all of the consequences. Get signed, written approval from your relatives if you have them test, to make sure that they understand what they are doing.

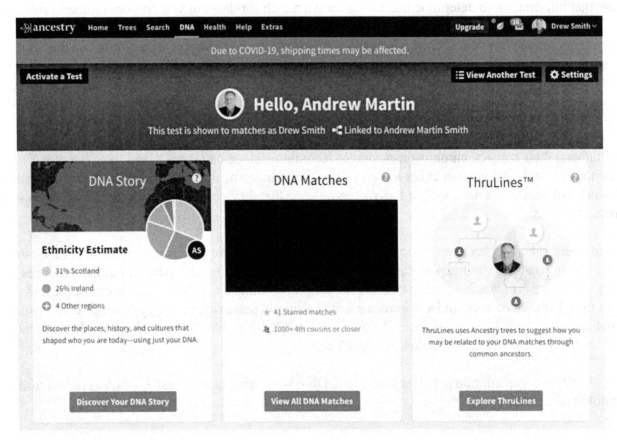

Figure 6.6: Ancestry DNA test results

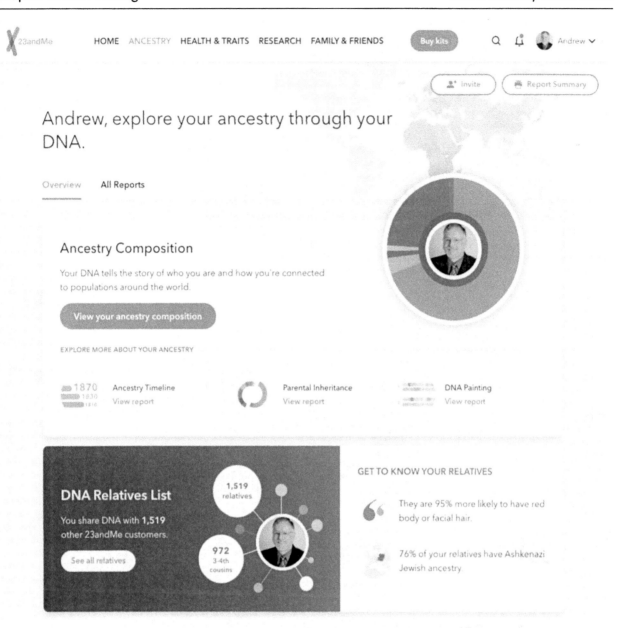

Figure 6.7: 23andMe DNA test results

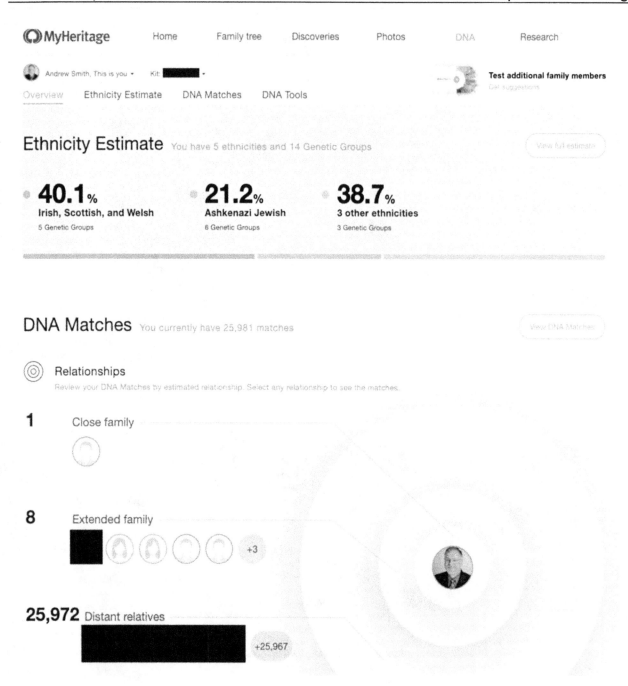

Figure 6.8: MyHeritage DNA test results

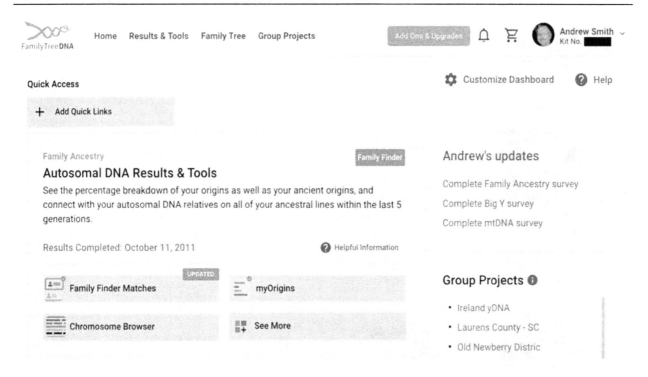

Figure 6.9: FamilyTreeDNA Family Finder (autosomal) DNA test results

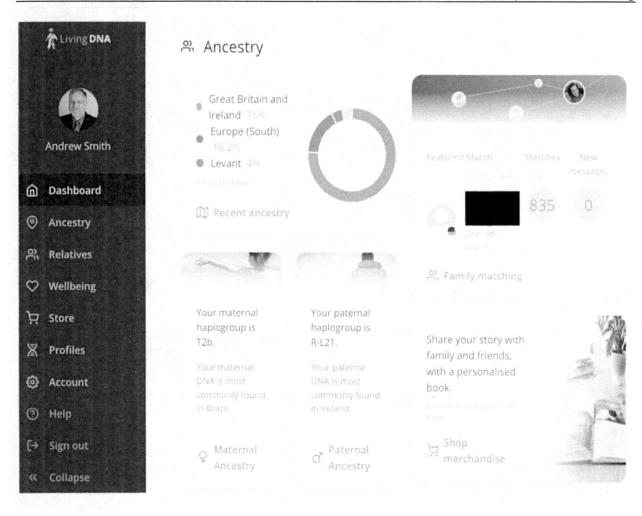

Figure 6.10: LivingDNA DNA test results

Chapter 7: Using Online Repositories

In Chapter 3 (the genealogical research process) you were introduced to the idea of online genealogical repositories, with the four largest being:

- FamilySearch
- Ancestry
- MyHeritage
- Findmypast

In this chapter, we'll discuss the best way to search for information within these repositories. Many of the ideas discussed in this chapter will also apply to any online repository of information.

As mentioned in Chapter 3, FamilySearch is free to use by anyone, although you must create a free account in order to search for records in it. Ancestry and MyHeritage provide versions designed for library patrons, so check with your local public library to see if it subscribes to the library edition for one or both of those repositories. Ancestry Library Edition is normally restricted to use within the library itself, while MyHeritage Library Edition may be used at home by accessing it through your library's website. Also investigate discounted Ancestry subscriptions for current U.S. college/university students and for members of AARP, if you would qualify for either of those.

Organization of information sources

When you last visited a public library or a bookstore, you may have noticed that the books are organized into genres: categories and subcategories (fiction divided into children's, young adult, mystery, science fiction/fantasy, romance, etc.; and non-fiction divided into history, biography, self-help, how-to, etc.). In the same way, sources of information in online genealogical repositories are organized into collections and collections into categories. Common categories of sources include:

- Vital records (birth, marriage, and death)
- Census
- Immigration
- Military
- Legal (wills, probate, and land)
- Newspapers

As a new genealogist, you may find it overwhelming to see so many different sources of information. You might be tempted simply to use the website's main search box and enter a name of an ancestor, just to see what comes up. The problem with that method is that you're likely to get a hodgepodge of records from many different collections, including collections that you're unfamiliar with. You're also likely to get a lot of hits for people with the same name as your ancestor, who lived in a different place or a different time than your ancestor. And while the search box may let you limit the places where and/or times when your ancestor lived, you'll still be jumping from one type of record to another. So how might you go about the process in a more organized fashion? Especially when you're still learning about the different record types and how they are used?

Catalogs

In the same way that mega-bookstores provide store layouts signs at their entrances showing what genres of books they have and where they are, the major online repositories provide online catalogs showing what types of collections they have and how to get to them. Collections are usually organized by place, date, and/or type.

FamilySearch

After you log in, choose Search from the top menu and then Records. You should see this:

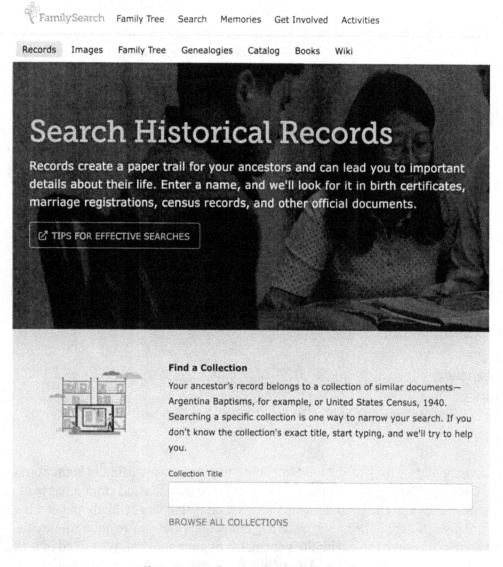

Figure 7.1: FamilySearch Search Records page

Then click "Browse All Collections" to see this:

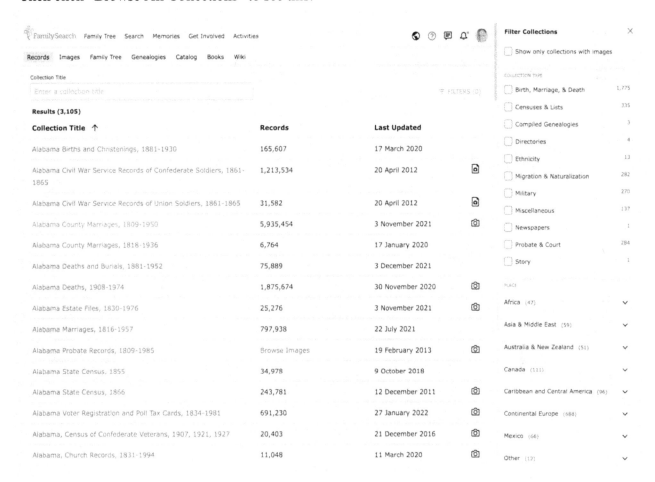

Figure 7.2: FamilySearch "Browse All Collections" page

Ancestry

To find Ancestry's searchable list of all collections, go to Search and then Card Catalog:

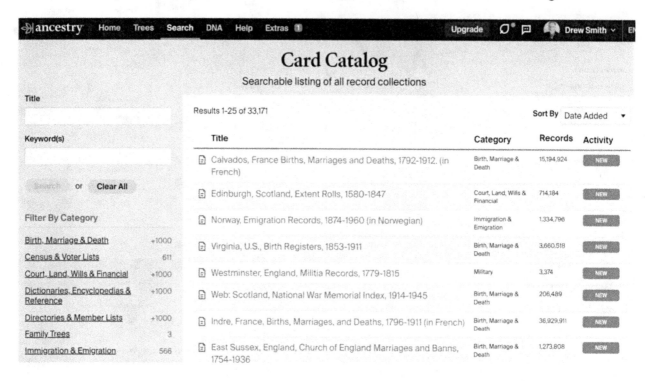

Figure 7.3: Ancestry Card Catalog

MyHeritage

To find MyHeritage's searchable list of all collections, go to Research and then Collection Catalog:

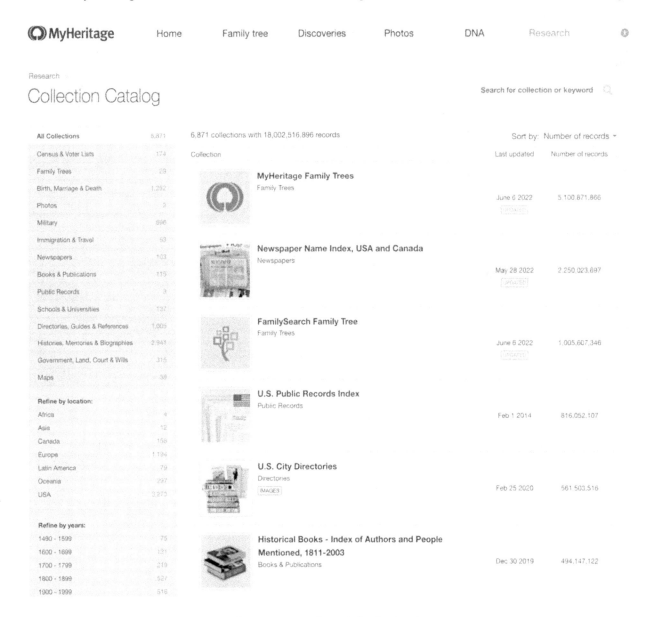

Figure 7.4: MyHeritage Collection Catalog

Findmypast

To find Findmypast's searchable list of all collections, go to Search and then "All record sets":

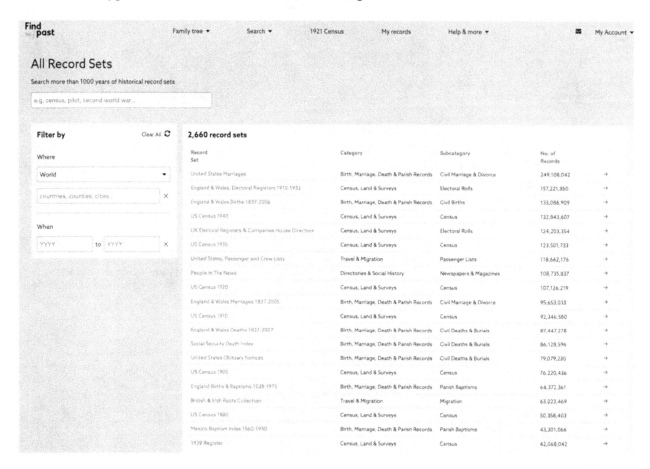

Figure 7.5: Findmypast All Records Sets

Selecting and searching a collection

Now that we know how to locate a particular collection in an online repository, let's find one and search it. We'll use FamilySearch as an example.

Let's assume that we're interested in finding a death record for our South Carolina ancestor who died after 1950. By clicking "Birth, Marriage, & Death", we can limit our search to the over 1700 collections that have that type of information source. Let's now narrow further to those that are for the geographic area of interest (South Carolina) and that are most recent (1950 to present):

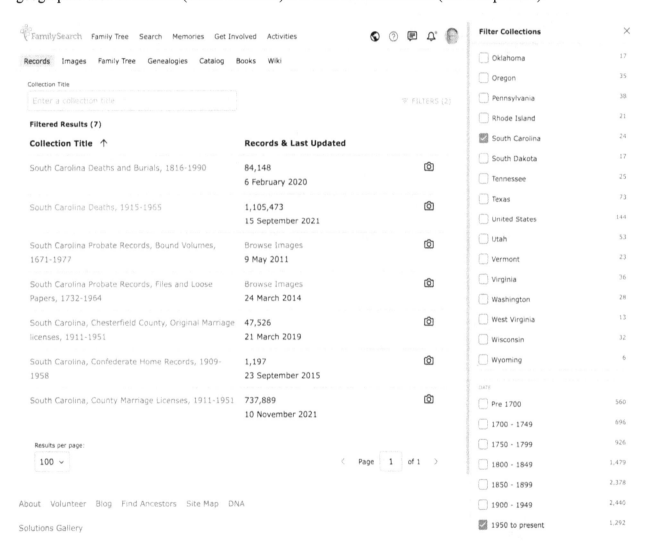

Figure 7.6: FamilySearch results page for a South Carolina record collection after 1950

We now see only two record collections that contain death records, and the much larger death record collection (the one from 1915-1965 with over 1 million records) looks like it will have a better chance of providing information about our ancestor, so I'll choose that one. Then I'll choose "More Options".

We now have a search page (see Figure 7.7 below) that we can use to try to find the specific person we're interested in. Let's look for my grandfather, George W. Martin, who died in the early 1960s:

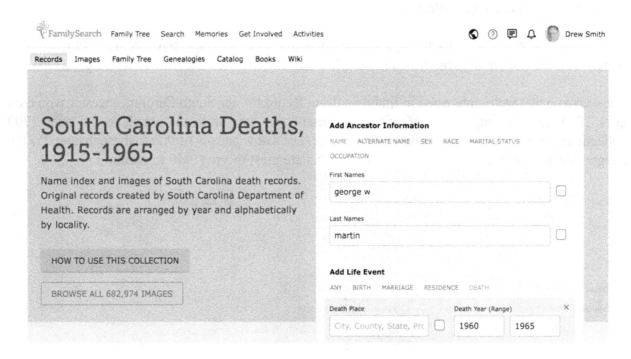

Figure 7.7: FamilySearch search page for South Carolina Deaths, 1915-1965

We get 459 results, of which my grandfather's death record is the first result:

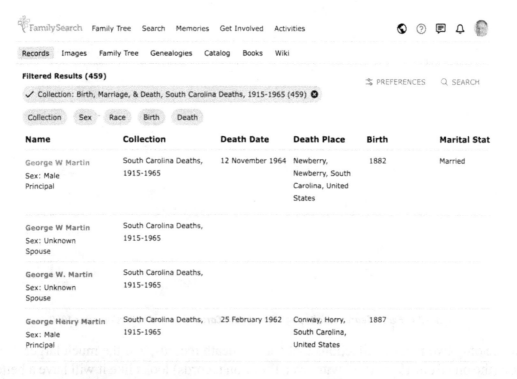

Figure 7.8: FamilySearch results page for the search for George W. Martin

Now I can scroll all the way to the far right and click the icon that looks like a camera (meaning "image") to see his actual South Carolina death certificate:

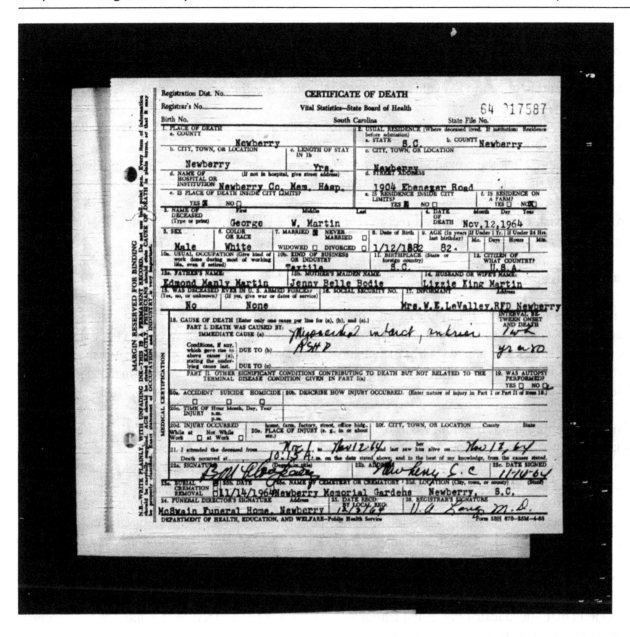

Figure 7.9: Death certificate for the author's maternal grandfather, George W. Martin

We'll discuss death certificates in detail in a later chapter, but the point of this exercise was to show how we can use an online repository's catalog (or equivalent) to find the best collection to search first. "George W. Martin" is a common name, so if I had used the repository's main search screen to look for information about my grandfather, I would probably have had to sort through millions of records that were about some other George W. Martin.

Download the document

Once you have found a relevant document in an online repository, be sure to download a copy of it to your own desktop or laptop computer (and then rename it and file it, as described in Chapter 4). After all, if you found the document on a subscription website, you may decide later not to subscribe to that particular site, and you don't want to lose access to the document.

On FamilySearch, click the Download link above the image at the top right.

On Ancestry, click the green Save button at the top right and choose "Save to your computer".

On MyHeritage, click the paired brackets at the top right of the image, then click the download icon (between the printer icon and the "Exit full screen" button).

On Findmypast, click the download record icon just to the right of the printer icon at the top right of the screen.

Search strategies and problems

Search boxes tempt us to fill in lots of information. They allow us to put in all the parts of the name, specific places, and specific years. They may let us add the names of our ancestor's relatives, such as the names of spouses or parents. The risk is that we may enter incorrect information. What if the death certificate didn't include a middle name or middle initial? What if the person died in a different state? What if they died in an earlier or later year?

When searching for information, we must make judgments as to what we're relatively certain of, and what we're not. If we get too many results, we may need to narrow our search. If we get too few results, or none at all, we may need to broaden our search. As you become more experienced, you'll become more skilled at how much to broaden or narrow your search.

One of the factors that can help us decide how much information to include in a search is how common the ancestor's name is. Common names like "George W. Martin" may require adding enough information to narrow the search to a particular place at a particular time. (The same goes for my other grandfather, William Smith.) But what if the name is more unusual? In that case, you may be able to do a search using only the name (such as for my grandmother, Rachel Weinglass). However, another wrinkle is that unusual first name and surnames may be mis-transcribed or mis-indexed, so you may have to be creative in how you spell the name when doing the search. Learn to "creatively misspell" your ancestor's name.

We also must realize that the record may simply not exist. But if it does, perhaps that particular collection hasn't been fully digitized or if it has, hasn't been indexed. Or perhaps our ancestor's name was mis-indexed. We may have to resort to browsing to find it.

Browsing vs. searching

Some collections are easier to browse than others. The South Carolina Death collection that we searched does allow us to browse its over 680,000 images, but the pieces of that collection are not conveniently labeled for browsing. Let's look at a different collection that is a bit easier to browse: the 1920 U.S. census.

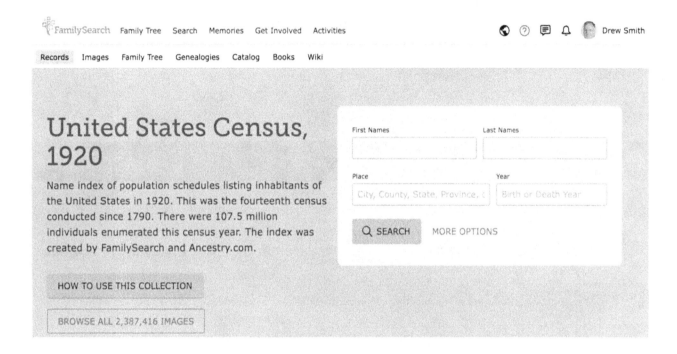

Figure 7.10: FamilySearch search page for the 1920 U.S. census

Notice the browse button. If I click that, I can narrow it to a particular state, then to a particular county, and then to a particular part of the county. I believe that my mother was born in Moon Township in Newberry County, South Carolina, so I'll click the link to browse that particular collection:

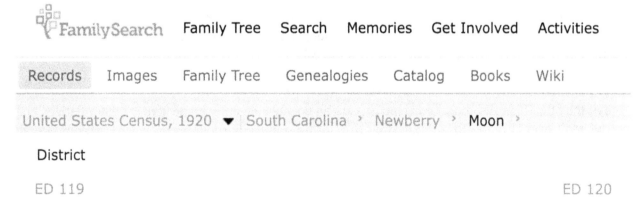

Figure 7.11: FamilySearch browse page for Moon Township, Newberry County, South Carolina in the 1920 U.S. census

I see two different census enumeration districts: ED 119 and ED 120 (don't worry, we'll explain those when we get to a later chapter on doing census research). Since I don't know which one might have my Martin grandparents and their children, I'll probably have to browse both of them. Let's see how many records I'm going to have to browse:

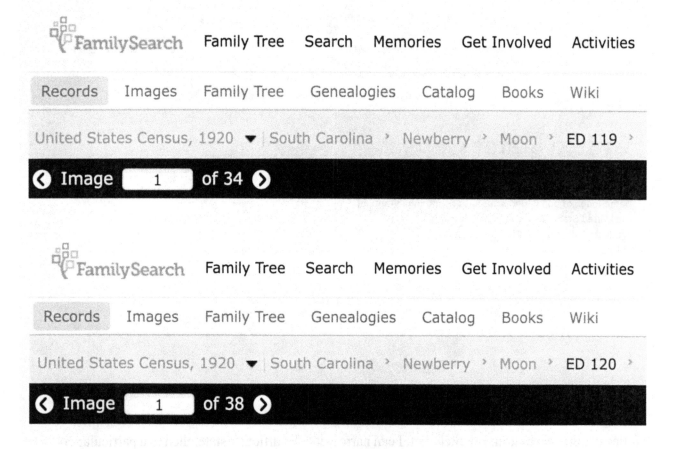

Figures 7.12 and 7.13: FamilySearch headers for Enumeration Districts 119 and 120

Not bad. Only 72 images in total. I can scan through those in a few minutes. In ED 119, at the top of image 13, I find my grandparents and their six oldest children. (My mother, the youngest of seven, wasn't born until later the same year.) See Figure 7.14 on the next page for the image of the census page.

One of the other benefits about browsing is that you may accidentally come across other relatives that you weren't even looking for or expecting to find! So don't ignore browsing when a search fails to turn up anything useful.

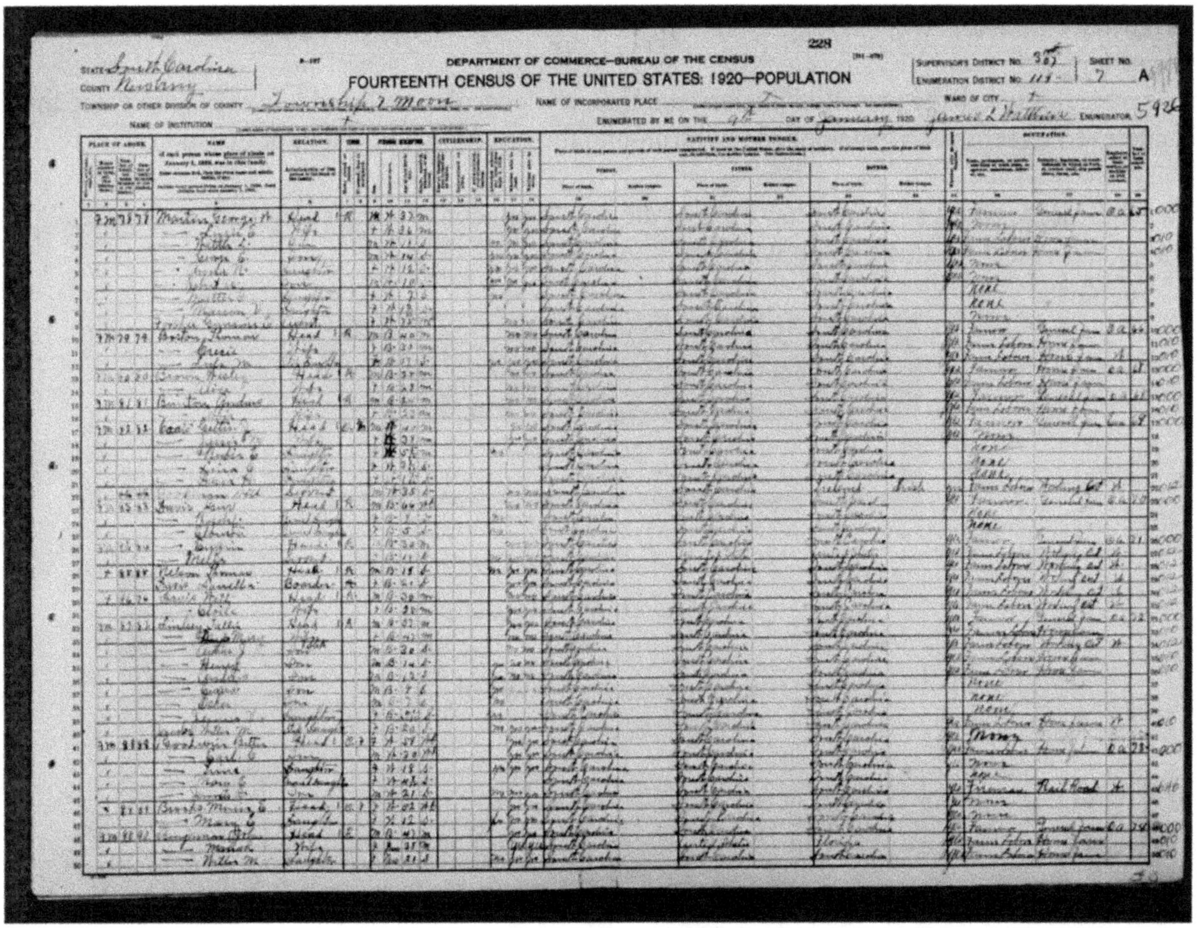

Figure 7.14: FamilySearch image of the 1920 U.S. census with the author's maternal grandparents and their children

Getting help

The big genealogy website providers understand that new genealogists need lots of help in using their sites, and even experienced genealogists will run into the occasional problem or question.

On FamilySearch, you'll see at the top right of the screen an icon of a question mark in a circle. Click that and you'll see this pop-up window:

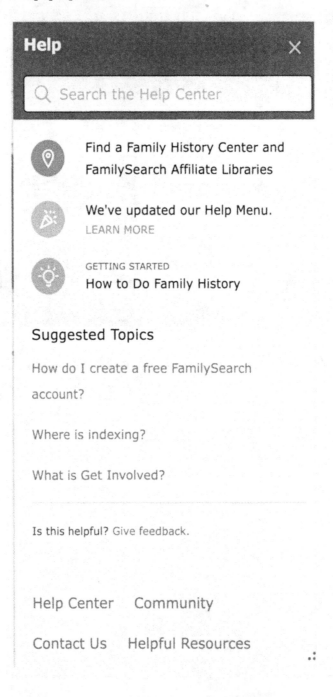

Figure 7.15: FamilySearch pop-up Help window

On Ancestry, you'll see Help at the top:

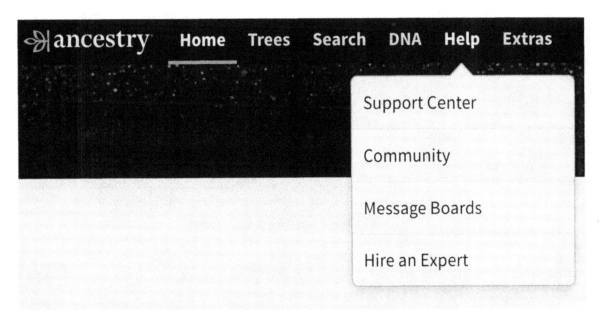

Figure 7.16: Ancestry Help menu

On MyHeritage, it's the combination of the circled question mark and the word Help:

Figure 7.17: MyHeritage Help menu

And on Findmypast, it's "Help & more":

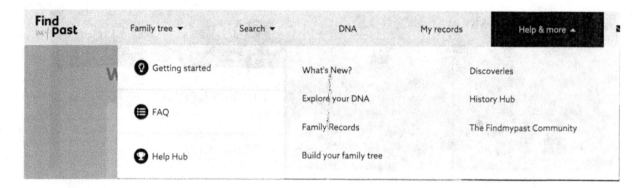

Figure 7.18: Findmypast "Help & more" menu

No matter which website you are using, don't be shy about getting help from the website's help documents.

Part II

Generation by Generation:

Doing the Research

Chapter 8:
Generations after 1950 in the U.S.

Begin by looking for information that was produced after April 1950. Why after April 1950? You'll discover in the next chapter that the U.S. federal census is taken every 10 years and then released to the public after 72 years. This means that the 1950 census, which was originally taken in April 1950, became available to the public on 1 April 2022. In many ways, the availability of the U.S. census dramatically changes how you do genealogical research. So, this means that you have to use records *other* than U.S. census records when you are trying to document all of the events of the lives of those who were living after 1 April 1950.

The information you'll be looking at will usually include information about yourself (and any of your descendants), your siblings (if you have any) and their descendants, and perhaps your parents and grandparents. Depending on your own age, there may even be information about earlier generations. For me, none of my great-grandparents lived past 1944, so my search for post-1950 information is about just me and my brother and the two generations before him and me (our parents and our grandparents).

Home sources

According to an old proverb, home is where the heart is. It's also where the genealogical documents are that you need to look for and start with. You, your parents, or other relatives may have collected items that contain genealogical information. You'll be looking for such things as:

- Letters
- Diaries and journals
- Photographs (hopefully with identifying info written on the back)
- Scrapbooks
- Address books
- Newspaper clippings (including obituaries)
- Birth, marriage, or death certificates
- Legal documents, such as wills and probated estates
- Church annuals and bulletins
- School yearbooks and other school records (you saved your report cards, right?)
- Artifacts (linens, jewelry, other inherited items)

You'll want to examine your entire home, including file cabinets, desk drawers, closets, attics, basements, garages, and off-site storage units, since home sources of genealogical info could end up pretty much anywhere. And if your relatives are alive and permit it, you'll want to work with them to do the same thing for their own homes.

As you find items, scan the paper documents and photographs, and take photos of the artifacts.

What you and your living relatives know and remember, including social media

Besides the physical reminders of your families found in your homes, you carry around personal memories. You may have been present for births, marriages, deaths, and burials, and for church and school events.

Beyond this, there is so much more that you remember but that you'll probably need a few suggestions to bring those memories to mind. Search online for lists of questions that you can ask yourself and your relatives. These will include such things as:

- Where did your family live? What was each house like?
- What kinds of food did your family prepare?
- What kinds of music, movies, radio shows, and TV shows did your family enjoy?
- Did you have pets?
- Where did your family go on vacations?
- What kinds of games did your family play as children?
- What kinds of jobs did your family hold?
- Where did your family go to school? What were their favorite subjects?
- What holidays did your family celebrate, and how?

These are just examples of the kinds of questions that you should think about (the lists you'll find online will cover a lot more, so look for them). As you ask yourself these questions, and then ask other members of your family, record everyone's answers (ideally, at least with an audio recording, but even better, with a video recording). Assure your interviewees that you will not publish any of this information online for others to see, but that you will keep it only within your own notes.

As you discover new cousins in the course of your genealogical research, return to this section to see if you would want to do the same interviews with them. They may have memories of their parents, grandparents, or great-grandparents that you don't already have access to.

If your relatives use social media (such as Facebook), you might visit their pages to see what things they are most interested in. They may have documented important recent events in their lives or those of their immediate family (the births of children/grandchildren, birthdays, marriages, deaths, illnesses, vacations, graduations, new jobs, retirements, and so forth).

Newspapers

Once you have exhausted assembling and recording the home sources and personal memories of yourself and your close relatives, it's time for you to move into some traditional genealogical research processes, starting with newspapers. Newspapers have been around in the United States since it began, and before that in the British America colonies since 1690. So, you'll want to return to looking for newspapers for every chapter after this. But let's start with what newspapers can tell you about the events of your ancestor's lives in the post-1950 time period.

Obituaries and other death-related information

Probably the most useful source of information that you can find in a newspaper is an obituary. The obituary may include the following information for the deceased:

- Their full name and where they lived (usually just the city)
- A photo
- Their age at death
- Their birth date and location
- Places they may have lived
- Their marriage date and location and name of spouse
- Their death date and location
- The cause of death
- The names of their parents (including their mother's maiden name)
- Their occupation and employer
- Education (usually just post-secondary)
- Military service
- The names of organizations they may have been members of, including religious congregations
- The names and city locations of their survivors (spouse, parents, siblings, children, grandchildren, and sometimes others)
- The date and location of the planned memorial service, including dates/hours of visitation with the family beforehand
- The name of the funeral home
- The planned burial location
- The names of actual and honorary pall bearers
- Suggestions of where to send flowers or donations

Earlier obituaries tend to contain a lot more information than later ones, in part because newspapers that originally didn't charge for obituaries or that charged very little changed their practices and made the word count for obituaries very expensive.

In addition to traditional obituaries, you may also find *death notices* (very brief indications that someone has died, sometimes with a full obituary to follow in a later newspaper), and *funeral notices* (usually on the same date or on a date after the obituary), which focus on the details (date/time and location) of the funeral. Funeral notices may be repeated over multiple days, to make sure that people are able to see them.

Other info in newspapers

While obituaries may be the most common (and sometimes most useful) item that might appear in a newspaper about your family, you'll also want to look for:

- Birth announcements
- Marriage announcements
- Wedding anniversaries
- Accidents and illnesses
- Social visits and events
- School news
- Military news
- Business news
- Legal issues (crimes, lawsuits)
- Political news
- Letters to the editor
- Feature stories

Identifying newspapers

You need to identify what newspapers you want to search, based on where and when your family lived. Start by visiting the *Chronicling America* website, produced by the Library of Congress. You'll want to use its *U.S. Newspaper Directory*, located at this address:

https://chroniclingamerica.loc.gov/search/titles/

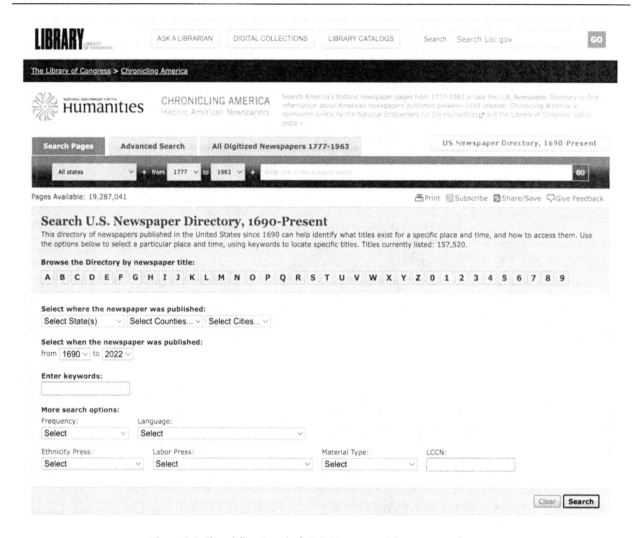

Figure 8.1: Chronicling America's U.S. Newspaper Directory search page

This will tell you what newspapers were published in each city, during each time period. In some cases, newspapers were discontinued, or they were merged into other newspapers. In major cities, there was often both a morning newspaper and an evening newspaper, but over the decades, almost all evening newspapers ceased publication.

Note that some newspapers may have been published for a particular ethnic audience. For instance, in Tampa, there is an African American newspaper and a Spanish-language newspaper. You can search for these in the *U.S. Newspaper Directory.*

The format and cost of accessing newspapers

Newspapers that still exist in some format can be divided into five categories:

- Newspapers that are not available anywhere online, but instead are only on microfilm
- Newspapers that have been scanned and made available online for free
- Newspapers that have been scanned and made available online for a cost
- Newspapers that were "born digital" and made available online for free
- Newspapers that were "born digital" and made available online for a cost

The *U.S. Newspaper Directory* will tell you which repositories hold copies of the newspaper, and in what format. In every U.S state, there is a central repository (usually a large university library, but sometimes a state library, state archive, state historical society, or large public library) that keeps a microfilm copy of all known newspapers for that state. If the microfilm has not been scanned and put online, you would have to visit the repository that holds the microfilm and view it for yourself, or you would need to contact the repository to see if they would look up information for you and perhaps scan an article to send to you.

Chronicling America is a free site with a lot of newspapers, but only a small percentage of its content is going to be less than 95 years old, due to copyright restrictions. Other free (as well as paid) newspaper sites can be found at the General Resources subcategory of the Newspapers category of *Cyndi's List*, at https://www.cyndislist.com/newspapers

Three major commercial websites provide online access via subscription to scanned U.S. newspapers:

- Newspapers.com (a service of Ancestry.com), in particular its Publisher Extra edition for more current newspapers
- GenealogyBank (a service of NewsBank)
- NewspaperArchive

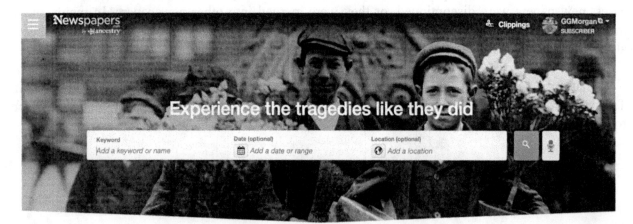

Figure 8.2: Newspapers.com search screen

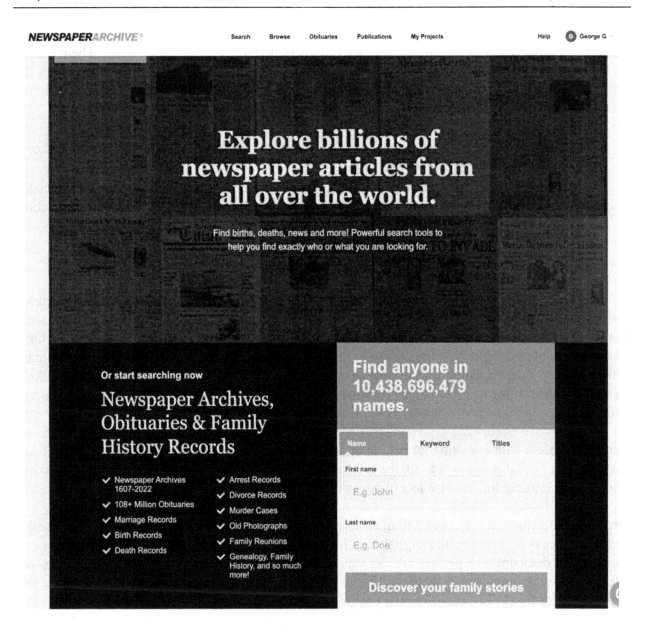

Figure 8.3: NewspaperArchive home page

Before spending any money to subscribe to any newspaper database:

1. Check the database first to see if it actually carries newspapers for the places and times where your family lived.
2. Check to see whether your local public library already provides you with access to the database. Many libraries provide access to Newspapers.com, and many provide access to subsets of GenealogyBank (America's GenealogyBank or HeritageHub, previously known as America's Obituaries & Death Notices).

More recent newspapers may have been "born digital", meaning that their text was actually originally typed into a computer before the newspaper was produced and printed. Newspapers began being "born digital" in the 1990s, although smaller newspapers may not have gone the computer route until the 2000s. Sites with "born digital" newspapers usually include only the text of the newspaper and may not include any photos. You can usually find these newspapers at two types of locations:

- A general newspaper database that your local public library may subscribe to, such as Access World News (a service of NewsBank)
- A site maintained by the newspaper itself, which may either be free or have a cost associated with it. You'll need to check the newspaper's own website to see how far back their archive goes.

Searching within newspapers

Unlike some of the genealogy-specific databases that were discussed in the previous chapter, newspaper databases are not designed specifically for genealogists. Even if the newspaper database is marketed toward genealogists and has a place for you to enter a first name and last name for searching, what is really happening is that the database is taking those two parts of the name and creating a phrase with them, and then searching for that phrase in the full text of the database. (It may also be looking for the two parts of the name separated by one other word, which allows for a middle name or middle initial.)

Another problem with searching for people in newspaper databases is when part of the name is also a common English-language word. So, the results you get may include not only pages with the people who are you looking for, but also lots of pages that aren't relevant to your search.

Finally, a problem with searching within newspapers that were originally printed and then digitized is that the process of creating the digital text for searching (known as *OCR*, for *optical character recognition*) does not do a perfect job. Newspapers were never designed for long-term storage, and over time the ink making up a word may bleed into the surrounding paper just a bit, causing the text to be a little bit fuzzy. This can cause the OCR process to produce incorrect text. So don't be surprised if your family is named in a newspaper but the newspaper database doesn't pull up the right pages.

As you go through later chapters of this book, remember to look for your ancestors in newspapers, all the way back to the time of Colonial America.

Vital records (birth, marriage, and death)

The word *vital* has many meanings, and we may think of one of its most common meanings: "very important". But it also has the meaning of "pertaining to the facts of life, such as birth, marriage, and death". In genealogy, we speak of *vital records* as being that set of records that concern those significant aspects of a person's life, in particular those recorded by government agencies.

In the United States, vital records are not kept at the national level (as they are in many other countries), but instead are maintained by individual U.S. states, and they may even be recorded by individual counties (who keep their own copy but send a copy to their state office of vital records). This means that you will need to search individual state collections of birth, marriage, and death records, and in some cases, you may have to contact the relevant county to get an actual copy of the record.

To find vital records for a particular U.S. state, use the FamilySearch Research Wiki. You'll find a good starting page at https://www.familysearch.org/en/wiki/United_States_Vital_Records

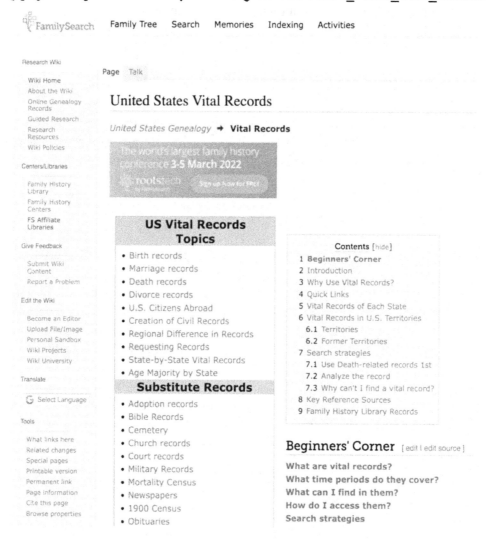

Figure 8.4: FamilySearch Research Wiki page for United States Vital Records

Restrictions

The release of birth, marriage, and death records to the general public may be restricted by state law, in order to preserve privacy. In some cases, access to the more recent records may require that the person asking for the record is either the person the record is about or an immediate family member, such as a child or grandchild.

Typically, birth records are under the longest restrictions (don't be surprised if they are restricted if they are less than 75, 100, or even 125 years old).

In some states, marriage certificates are considered public records and have no time limits, but in other states, they may not be made available for 50 years.

Death records are sometimes restricted for at least 50 years.

Older records are often released to the public without restriction.

Religious records

Government-produced and maintained vital records are often known as *civil records*, as opposed to other types of records, such as religious records. If someone marries in a house of worship, the religious institution may have a record of their marriage (completely separate from the one kept by the local government). Although religious bodies may not directly record births or deaths, they may record baptisms/christenings and funerals/burials. We'll cover religious records in detail in the next chapter.

Burial records (funeral homes and cemeteries)

When a relative dies, there may be a number of records that are generated apart from the official government death certificate (and any newspaper obituary). Funeral homes may keep records, although because these are privately-owned companies, they may or may not be willing to share information with genealogists. Cemeteries, too, may have their own sets of records in their own offices, especially if the cemetery is large. If you can learn the name of the funeral home and/or the name of the cemetery that handled your relative's burial, you may be able to contact them for information.

If you do not know where exactly your relative was buried (even after checking for death certificates or obituaries), you may be able to use several large websites to see if the burial site was added to their database. The three largest databases for cemetery records are:

- Find a Grave (findagrave.com)
- BillionGraves (billiongraves.com)
- Interment.Net (interment.net)

Find a Grave

Find a Grave has over 210 million memorials and is owned by Ancestry.com. Its contents have been contributed by volunteers who have visited over 532,000 cemeteries around the world, including over 411,000 in the United States. In most of these cases, the volunteers have taken photos of the grave markers.

While you can go to the Find a Grave website in order to search it directly, you can also search its index as a collection at both FamilySearch and Ancestry.

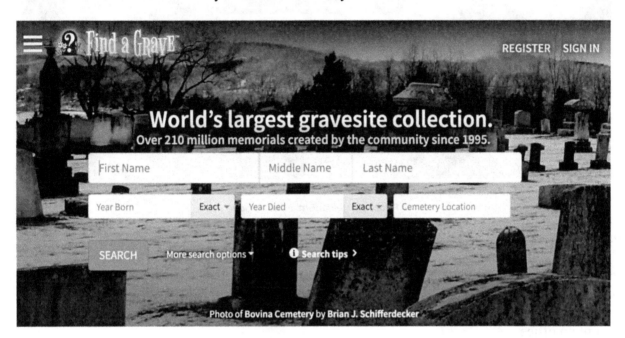

Figure 8.5: Find a Grave home page

BillionGraves

BillionGraves has over 28 million records. Much smaller in size than Find a Grave, BillionGraves differs from Find a Grave in that it provides a free app to volunteers to record not only the photos of the grave markers, but also the exact location of the grave using GPS coordinates. This makes it easier to go directly to the gravesite if you wanted to visit the cemetery.

While you can go to the BillionGraves website in order to search it directly, you can also search its index as a collection at both FamilySearch and MyHeritage. Its records for the United States, Canada, England, Scotland, Wales, Ireland, Australia, and New Zealand can also be searched at Findmypast.

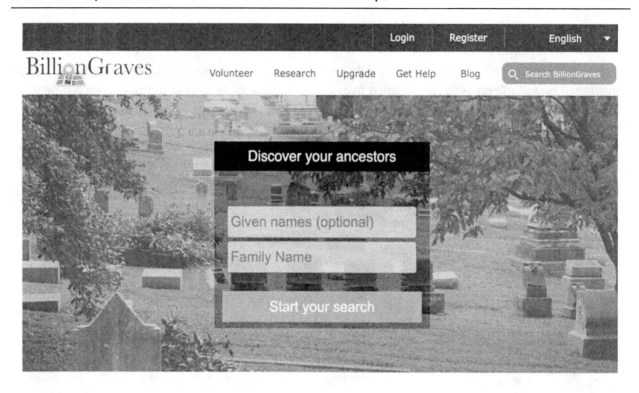

Figure 8.6: BillionGraves home page

Interment.Net

Interment.Net differs from both Find a Grave and BillionGraves in that the information in its database does not come from crowdsourcing (volunteers putting in the information themselves), but instead from single sources for each cemetery, such as a government agency, cemetery office, or religious institution office.

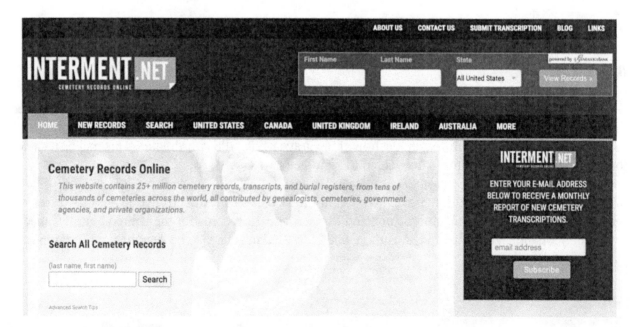

Figure 8.7: Interment.net

School yearbooks

College and high school yearbooks (also known as annuals) have been around since the early 1800s, but they may be an especially good source of information for your relatives in the post-1950 era. While your relatives may own copies of their own yearbooks, you may also find copies at public and academic libraries. Ancestry.com has a collection entitled *U.S., School Yearbooks, 1900-1999*, containing more than 450,000 yearbooks, more than 62 million pages, and nearly 730 million entries.

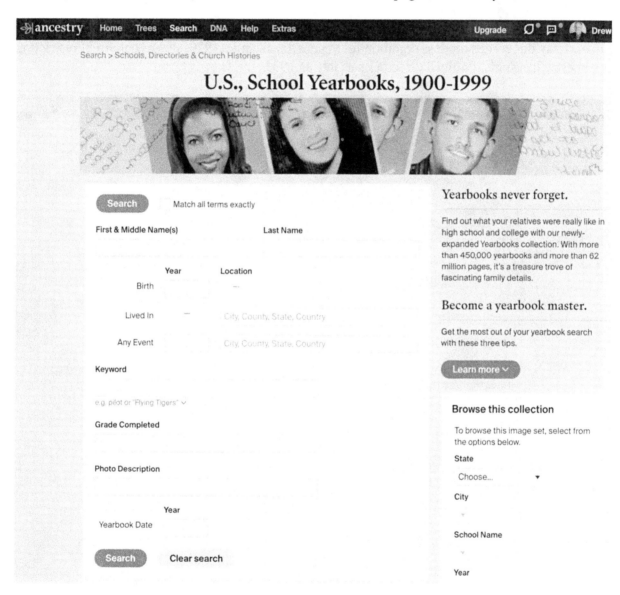

Figure 8.8: Ancestry's U.S. School Yearbooks search screen

City directories

In the United States, city directories have been around since the late 1700s, but they are especially useful for research in the 1800s and 1900s. We'll be getting to the U.S. federal censuses in the next chapter, but it's worth noting now that city directories have the advantage of being produced usually every year (not just in 10-year intervals) and can cover years in the last half of the twentieth century when census records have not yet been released to the public.

Public and academic libraries often hold print copies of city directories for their geographic areas. Digitized city directories are less common for years after the mid-1920s due to copyright restrictions, but Ancestry has some digitized directories as late as 1995.

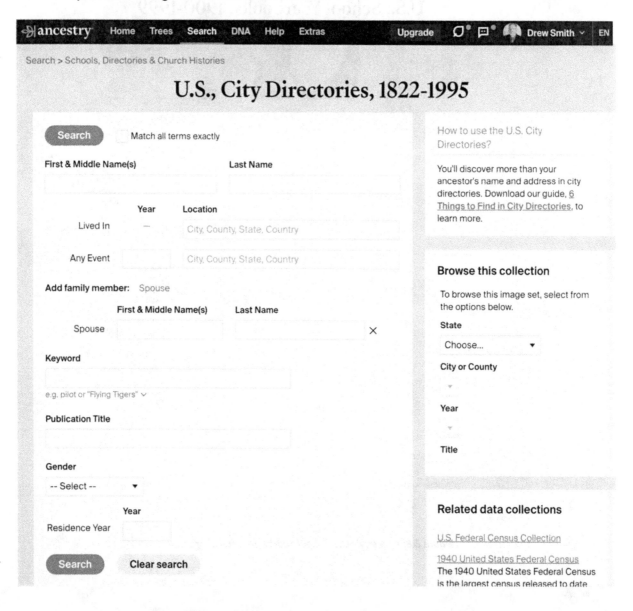

Figure 8.9: Ancestry's U.S. City Directories search screen

City directories normally list only adults and their residential address, and may list just the head of household and, if a married male, the name of his wife. In some cases, a widow's entry may also name her late husband. The individual's occupation is often given, and in some cases, addresses may be given for both the business and the home.

Some directories, in additional to providing an alphabetical list of residents, may also list residents by street address, which is helpful when trying to figure out who your relative's neighbors were.

Telephone directories (phone books)

Telephone directories, usually divided into *white pages* for individuals and *yellow pages* for businesses, can be a helpful resource for research into your twentieth-century relatives. Public libraries may keep print copies of older directories for their local areas. Ancestry has telephone directories for the 1993–2002-time frame. Like city directories, telephone directories can help to identify exactly where your relatives were living in certain years.

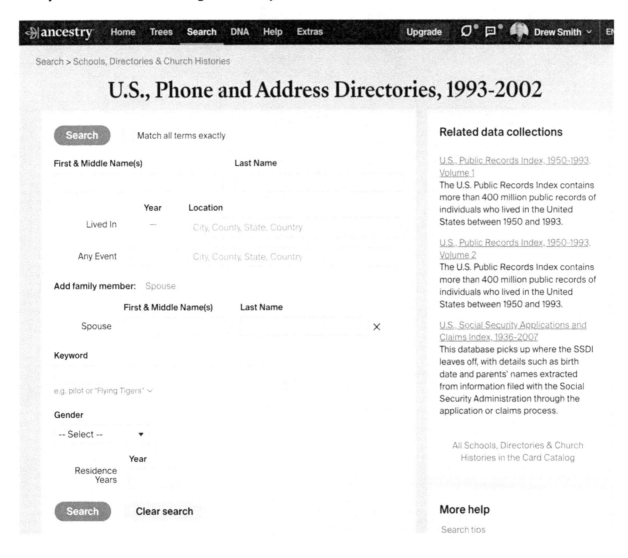

Figure 8.10: Ancestry's U.S. Phone and Address Directories search screen

Chapter 9:
Generations from 1880 to 1950 in the U.S.

In the last chapter, we covered home sources, personal memory, newspapers, vital records, burial records, school yearbooks, city directories, and telephone directories. All of those types of records will continue to be important as you move your research back to 1950 and earlier.

In some cases, some of those records will be easier to research in earlier time periods, because U.S. newspapers more than 95 years old will be in the public domain (no longer under copyright restrictions), and many vital records may be old enough to no longer be under privacy restrictions.

But there are some additional record types that you will want to explore for this earlier time. So let's look at records that will be especially useful for relatives living at least a part of their lives between 1880 and 1950. For me, this includes my parents, my 4 grandparents, my 8 great-grandparents, and even a few of my great-great-grandparents.

This chapter introduces the U.S. federal census, U.S. state censuses, military records from World War II and World War I, immigration and naturalization records, church records, and probate records.

U.S. Federal Census (1880-1950)

Why and how

National governments have counted the sizes of their populations for centuries. One of the earliest uses of a census was for the government to know how many men of an appropriate age were available to call up for military duty. As some nations became governed by democratically elected representatives, censuses became important for knowing how many representatives each area of the population was entitled to. The United States, since its founding, has been no exception. Fortunately, for genealogists with ancestors in the U.S., censuses can provide a wealth of details about individuals.

If you're an adult, you should be old enough to remember at least one U.S. federal census enumeration, if not several. This is because the United States government conducts a census of the U.S. population once every 10 years, as required by the U.S. Constitution. In its most basic form, the census tries to identify how many people are living within each U.S. state, within each county, and within smaller geographic areas known as *enumeration districts*. The enumeration enables the determination of how many U.S. Congressional representatives each state gets and allows state governments to draw appropriate congressional boundaries so that individual representatives represent the same-sized population (approximately) as every other in that same state.

The United States Census Bureau, now part of the Department of Commerce, has been responsible for conducting the census enumeration since 1902. Prior to 1902 and back to 1840, an agency known as the Census Office was responsible for the census. Between 1790 and 1870, the census was taken by U.S. Marshals (individuals who were part of federal law enforcement), but after the passage of an 1879 act of Congress, specially trained individuals, officially known as *census enumerators* (informally referred to as "census takers"), were hired to conduct the census. Census enumerators were given a set of explicit instructions as to how to conduct the census and how to fill in each blank on the official census forms, known as *census schedules*. By reading those instructions, genealogists are better able to understand the meanings of what is being entered onto the census schedules.

https://www.census.gov/history/www/through_the_decades/census_instructions/

Enumerator's Reference Manual

The following paragraphs on population and housing items were extracted from the Enumerator's Reference Manual for the 1950 Census of the United States:

POPULATION ENUMERATION FORMS

The Population Schedule

61. *Population on front, Housing on back.*—The front of the Population and Housing Schedule (Form P1) contains spaces for information about people; a line is to be filled for each person living in your ED. The front of the schedule may be called separately the Population Schedule. The back contains spaces for information about the places in which they live; a line is to be filled for each dwelling unit or nondwelling-unit quarters. The back may be called separately the Housing Schedule.

62. *Arrangement of items.*—On the Population Schedule, questions 1 to 6 are to be answered for every household head, 7 to 14 for all persons, and questions 15 to 20c for persons 14 years of age and over. The questions at the bottom of the schedule are asked only for persons on the sample lines. Some of the sample questions are for all persons, some for persons 14 years of age and over.

Make entries first in items 1 to 6 for the head of the household. You will probably find it convenient to complete entries in items 7 to 14 for

all members of the household before starting items 15 to 20c. Items 15 to 20c (the employment items) are related and *must* all be asked of one person before going to the next person. Before leaving the Population side of the schedule, be sure that you have asked the appropriate sample questions for persons on the sample lines.

63. *Wording of questions.*—Ask the questions printed in *heavy type* in each item heading *exactly as they appear on the schedule.* The only exception is that the name or relationship of the person may be substituted for "this person" or "he." For example, "How old was Mr. Stone on his last birthday?" "Did your son do any work at all last week, not counting work around the house?"

64. *Space for notes.*—Space for notes has been provided on the schedule. On some schedules, this space is on the upper part, on others on the lower part, and on others in both places. Enter there the footnotes needed to explain unusual entries. Remarks explaining any irregular situation should be entered there.

Other forms

65. *Individual Census Report.*—This report is used for (1) certain classes of persons, who are not to be enumerated on the regular Population Schedule because they are nonresidents and (2) residents who should be enumerated on the regular Population Schedule, but whom you cannot interview personally. (See pars. 76, 77, and 264 to 272.)

66. *Infant Card.*—This card is to be filled out for each infant enumerated who was born in January, February, or March, 1950. (See pars. 273 to 275.)

67. *Special Agriculture Questionnaire.*—This questionnaire is to be filled by urban enumerators when they find one of the following in their ED's: a farm, a place of 3 or more acres, or a place having certain specialized agricultural operations. (See pars. 276 to 282.)

PERSONS TO ENUMERATE IN CENSUS OF POPULATION

Coverage

68. *Census date.*—The Census must count all persons living in the United States on April 1, 1950, and must count them where they usually live. All persons who were living on that date should be included and babies born after that date should be excluded.

69. *Usual place of residence.*—Enumerate every person at his "usual place of residence." This means, ordinarily, the place that he would name in reply to the question, "Where do you live?" or the place that he regards as his home. As a rule it will be the place where the person usually sleeps.

70. *Persons with no usual place of residence.*—Enumerate as part of the population of your ED persons with no usual place of residence, if they are in your ED at the time of enumeration.

71. *Nonresidents.*—Nonresidents are persons who are temporarily staying in

1-463

Figure 9.1: Part of the census enumerator instructions from the U.S. Census Bureau

Each census had an official *enumeration day*. Because it would take weeks (if not longer) to get to every household, the census enumerators were expected to record the information as of a particular date (meaning that a child born after that date was <u>not</u> counted, and any individual alive on that date but who died after that date <u>was</u> counted). Beginning with the 1930 census, the enumeration day has been April 1. However, it was June 1 in 1880, June 2 in 1890, June 1 in 1900, April 15 in 1910, and January 1 in 1920.

Types of information found in the 1880 to 1950 censuses

From its earliest times, the U.S. census has obtained more information than simply the number of people living in a particular place. When the census began in 1790, it recorded the names of the heads of the households (but not others) and categorized the number of individuals in each household by sex and age. By 1850, it began to add additional information, and once we get to 1880, we're looking at a long list of information recorded for each individual in the household. Let's look at the types of information collected between 1880 and 1950. Note that the order of information might vary from census to census.

Surnames: Except for the 1890 census, which separates into two lines the "Christian" (first or given) name from the surname (or last name), the entire name is always entered into the same box, normally with the surname appearing first. The enumerator may have spelled out the surname for each individual or may have simply drawn a line where the surname would go to indicate that the surname is the same as the last one shown above it.

First and middle names: In some cases, the enumerator provided only initials for the first and middle names; in other cases, the first name was spelled out, and it might be followed by a middle initial.

The informant: In 1940 (and only in 1940), a small circled "x" appears at the end of the name of one member of the household to indicate that this is the individual who provided the information to the census enumerator.

Relationship: The first person listed in the household is typically identified as the head (either left blank or the word "Head" used), and all other individuals are identified by their relationship to the head. Relatives living in the same household are identified as you would probably expect: wife, son, daughter, grandson, granddaughter, son-in-law, daughter-in-law, father, mother, brother, sister, brother-in-law, sister-in-law, uncle, aunt, nephew, niece, etc.

Unrelated individuals might also be living in the same household with the family. Examples of these are lodgers or boarders (lodgers usually pay only for the room, while boarders also get meals); inmates, which are not limited to our modern sense of prison inmates, but may include individuals living in schools, hospitals, poor houses, etc.; and other individuals, such as servants (maids, cooks, etc.).

Sex: The census normally used M for male and F for female.

Race: Prior to 1950, this column was usually labeled as "Color or Race". Depending upon the census year, census enumerators were given different instructions on how to record the color or race of the individuals being enumerated.

While whites were always recorded as "W", Blacks were recorded as "B" up through 1920 but "Neg" in censuses after that. After 1890, individuals of mixed race (white and Black) may have been recorded as Black or as "Mu" (for mulatto), but the 1890 census also distinguished those who were at least one-fourth Black ("quadroon") and those who were at least one-eighth Black ("octoroon").

Other abbreviations found in census schedules for the Race column are: "I" or "In" or "Ind" for Native American, "Mex" for Mexican, "C" or "Ch" or "Chi" for Chinese, "Jp" or "Jap" for Japanese, "Fil" for Filipino, "Hin" for Hindu, and "Kor" for Korean, with "Ot" used for any other race (the race was then written in the left-hand margin of the schedule). Not all of these abbreviations were used for all census years.

Age: Age is normally given in terms of the last birthday (even if they will gain another year the day following the census). Children less than 1 year old are normally recorded in terms of months (this is written as a fraction of 12, so a 6-month-old child will be recorded as 6/12). Some censuses also record a birth date (month and year).

Marital status: The census will normally indicate whether each individual is either single, married, divorced, or widowed. In some censuses, there may be an indication if the current marriage is not their first marriage (M2, M3, etc.), and in 1940, M7 is used if the person is married but their spouse is not living in the same household. Because of historical societal attitudes toward divorce, individuals may choose to tell the enumerator that they are married or widowed instead of divorced. The census may indicate how many years the individual has been married or may instead give their age as to when they first got married (even if it was a marriage previous to the current one).

Occupation: Depending upon the census year, the occupation information recorded may have consisted simply of the type of work or it may also have included a description of the type of business or industry for the worker. It may have also reported if the person was unemployed (and how many months or weeks), and whether the person was self-employed or working for someone else. Women who are not employed in an activity that makes money are usually recorded as "keeping house" or with similar language, or their occupation may be left blank or marked as "none". Children who are not already working a trade will frequently be recorded as "at home" or "at school" (or with similar language), or their occupation will be left blank.

Birthplace: Since 1850, censuses have asked where each individual was born. Typically, the enumerator would indicate the U.S. state (or territory) or if outside the U.S., the country. An entry of "Unknown" might appear in this column. Between 1880 and 1930, individuals were also asked where their father and their mother were born. For some censuses, enumerators were told to carefully distinguish between the English-speaking and French-speaking parts of Canada. Another issue that comes up with this column is that individuals were expected to identify the name of their birth country at the time of the census, not as it might have been named at the time when they were born. This means that your ancestor born in Poland might show up in later censuses as born in Poland (Russ.) or Russia.

Citizenship status: In many censuses starting with 1890, individuals born outside the United States were asked about their citizenship status: whether they were naturalized, or if not, whether they had taken out naturalization papers (sometimes labeled as "AL" for "alien". In 1890 and 1900, foreign-born individuals were asked how many years they had lived in the United States, and in 1900 and some later censuses, what year they had immigrated to the United States. In 1920, naturalized individuals were also asked what year they had naturalized.

Language and education: Depending upon the census, individuals were asked what language they spoke or simply whether or not they were able to speak English. They may have been asked whether they had attended school in the previous 12 months, and whether or not they could read and write. In 1940, individuals were asked to identify the highest grade of school that they had completed.

Health: In 1880 and 1890, individuals were asked about whether they were ill or disabled, and if so, what illness or disability they had. In 1880, 1890, and 1910, enumerators indicated if the individual was blind or deaf, and some of those censuses recorded other conditions, such as "idiotic", "insane", or "maimed/crippled/bedridden" (or otherwise disabled).

Home ownership (also called "tenure"): In 1890 and later, the head of household was asked whether the home was owned or rented (also called "hired"). If owned, a census might ask if the home was free of a mortgage or not. In 1930 and 1940, individuals were asked how much their home was worth (if owned) or how much their monthly rent was (if rented).

Other information: The 1900 and 1910 censuses asked women how many children they had had and of those, how many were still living. The 1940 census was unique (and is especially valuable for genealogists) because it also asked where individuals were living in 1935.

Locating copies of the U.S. Federal Census

Because of their extreme value to genealogical research, the U.S. federal censuses are among the types of records that you will find at the major genealogical websites, including FamilySearch (free), Ancestry (1880 and 1940 are free), MyHeritage, and Findmypast.

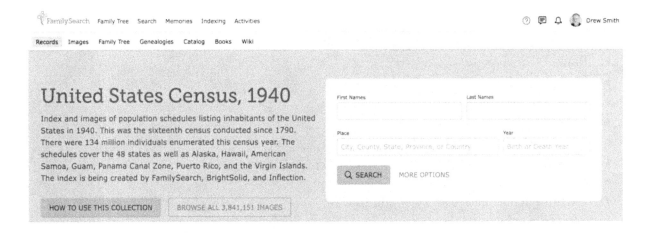

Figure 9.2: FamilySearch 1940 United State Census search screen

U.S. State and Territorial Censuses

Some (not all) U.S. states and territories conducted their own censuses. The most recent was 1945 in Florida, but the earliest were even earlier than the first U.S. federal census in 1790. These censuses are clearly valuable because:

- They may cover the years between the decennial federal census (many state censuses were conducted on years ending in 5, midway between the decennial censuses).
- They may help fill in the long gap between the 1880 and 1900 federal censuses.
- They may help make up for the loss of the U.S. federal census in specific states and counties.
- They sometimes asked questions that were not asked in the federal censuses.

Locating copies of U.S. state and territorial censuses

Most of these censuses can be found at FamilySearch (free), Ancestry, MyHeritage, and Findmypast. For more information about these censuses, read Ann S. Lainhart's 1992 book *State Census Records*.

Military Records – World War II and World War I

Between 1880 and 1950 the United States was involved in a number of different wars, but World War I and World War II generated an especially large number of records of use for genealogical research, including draft registration cards for both wars and army enlistment records for World War II.

World War II Army Enlistment Records

The U.S. World War II Army Enlistment Records (1938-1946) includes the following information on approximately 9 million men and women:

- Name
- Race
- Marital status (and indication of dependents, if any)
- Rank
- Birth year
- Birth state or country
- Citizenship status
- Residence (county and state)
- Education level (years)
- Civil occupation
- Enlistment date and place (city and state)
- Service number
- Branch of the service
- Component of the service
- Source
- Height (in inches)
- Weight (in pounds)

These records can be found at FamilySearch (free), Ancestry, MyHeritage, and Findmypast.

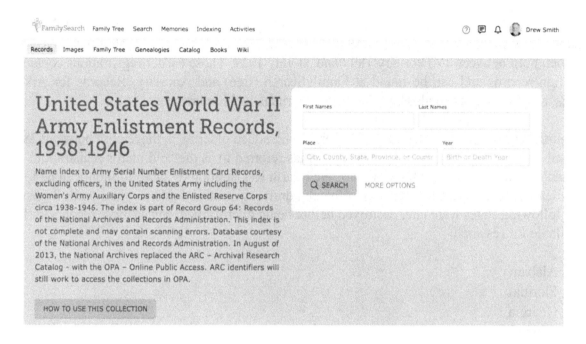

Figure 9.3: FamilySearch U.S. World War II Army Enlistment Records search screen

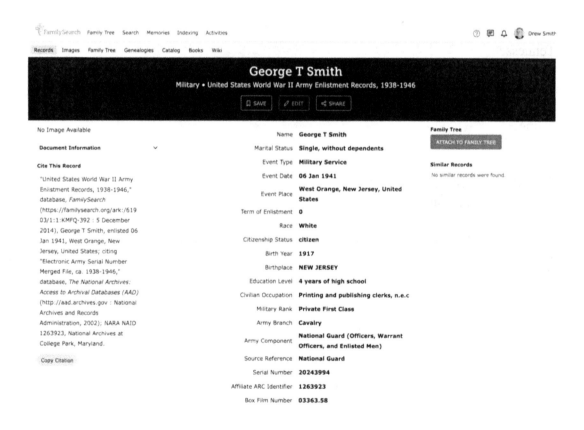

Figure 9.4: World War II Enlistment Record for the author's father, George T. Smith

World War II Draft Registration

A draft for World War II was signed into law on 16 September 1940. As a result, six different draft registrations were conducted between 1940 and 1942. The earlier draft registrations covered only those men born between 17 February 1897 and 31 July 1927. Those earlier registrations contain over 54 million records and can be found at FamilySearch (free) and Ancestry. Records for Arkansas, Georgia, and Louisiana can also be found at MyHeritage and Findmypast.

The Fourth Registration, conducted on 27 April 1942, added older men, those born between 28 April 1877 and 16 February 1897, and so it is sometimes referred to as the "old man's registration" or the "old man's draft". The available records for the Fourth Registration (over 15 million) can be found at FamilySearch (free) and Ancestry. Unfortunately, draft registration cards for the Fourth Registration for the following states were later destroyed before being microfilmed, and so those records will never be available for research:

- Alabama
- Florida
- Georgia
- Maine
- Mississippi
- New Mexico
- North Carolina
- South Carolina
- Tennessee

Information found on all draft registration cards (with a signature at the bottom) include:

1. Name
2. Place of residence
3. Mailing address
4. Telephone (exchange and number)
5. Age in years and date of birth
6. Place of birth (town or county, then state or country)
7. Name and address of person who will always know your address
8. Employer's name and address
9. Place of employment or business (number and street or RFD number, then town, county, and state)

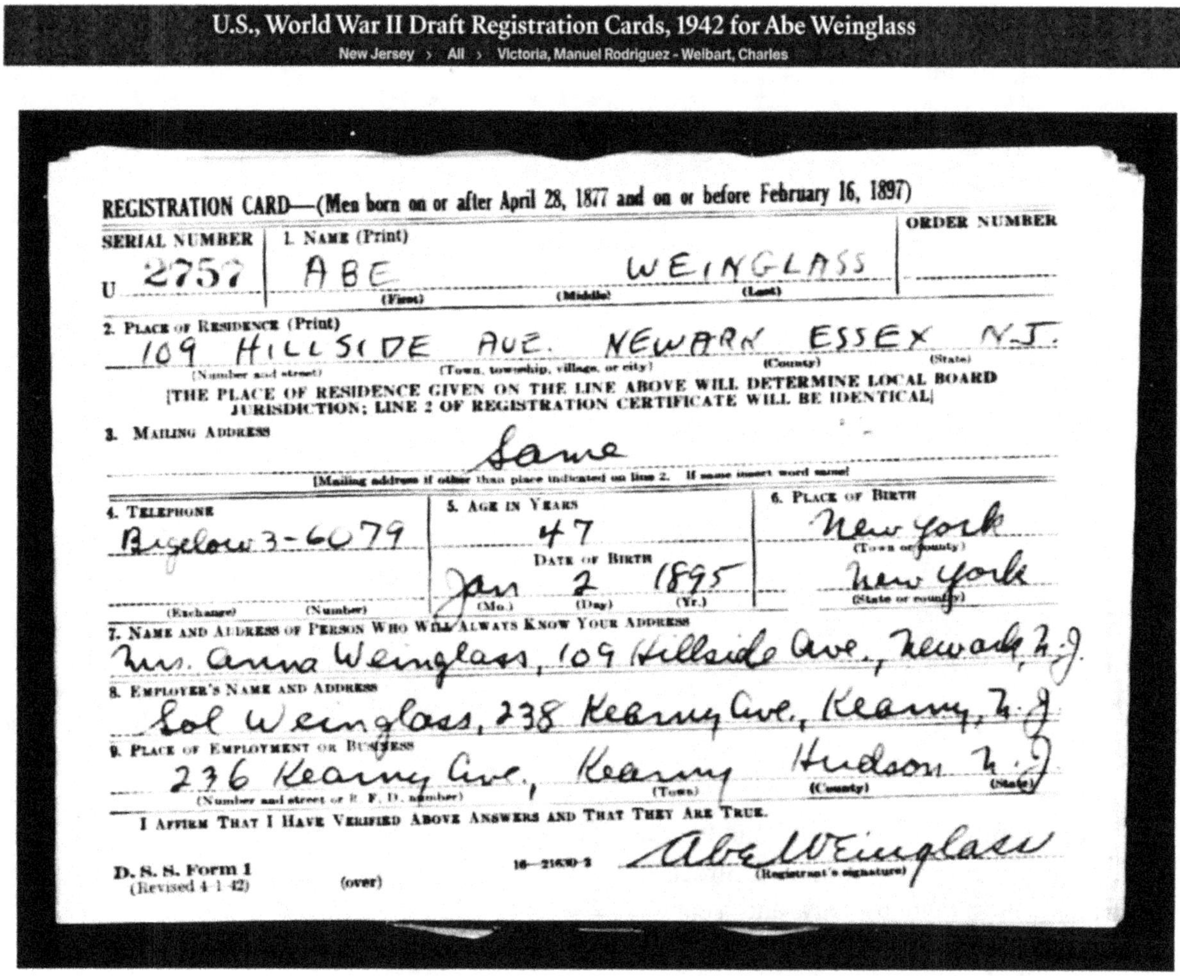

Figure 9.4: World War II draft registration card for the author's great-uncle, Abe Weinglass

World War I Draft Registration

After the United States declared war on Germany on 6 April 1917, the Selective Service Act of 1917 was signed into law on 18 May 1917. As a result, there were three draft registrations:

1. 5 June 1917 for men born between 5 June 1886 and 5 June 1896 (men who were between the ages of 21 and 31)
2. 5 June 1918 for men born between 6 June 1896 and 5 June 1897 (men who had turned 21 since the previous registration)
3. 12 September 1918 for men born between 12 September 1873 and 12 September 1900 (men between the ages of 18 and 45)

Although records for nearly 25 million men are recorded in the draft registrations, only about 2.8 million men were actually drafted into military service (in addition to the 2 million men who had volunteered). These records can be found at FamilySearch (free), Ancestry, MyHeritage, and Findmypast.

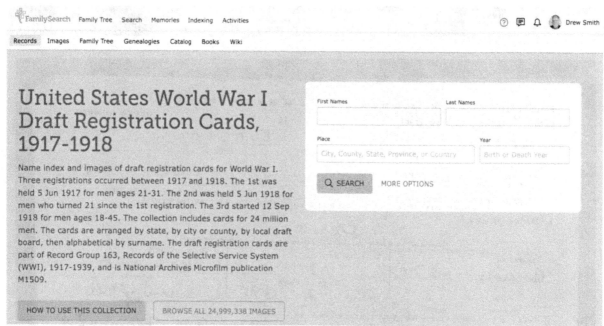

Figure 9.5: FamilySearch U.S. World War I Draft Registration Cards search screen

The following information can be found on the front of these draft registration cards, which is signed at the bottom:

1. Name in full ("Given name" and "Family name"), plus age in years
2. Home address (Street number, Street, City, and State)
3. Date of birth (Month, Day, and Year)
4. Are you (1) a natural-born citizen, (2) a naturalized citizen, (3) an alien, (4) or have you declared your intention (specify which)?
5. Where were you born? (Town, State, Nation)
6. If not a citizen, of what country are you citizen or subject?
7. What is your present trade, occupation, or office?
8. By whom employed? Where employed?
9. Have you a father, mother, wife, child under 12, or a sister or brother under 12, solely dependent on you for support (specify which)?
10. Married or single (which)?
11. What military service have you had? Rank, branch, years, Nation or State
12. Do you claim exemption from draft (specify grounds)?

The corner at the bottom left of the card had these instructions for the registrar: "If person is of African descent tear off this corner". While this instruction wasn't always followed, it frequently was.

The back of the card, entitled "Registrar's Report", included this at the top:

1. Tall, medium, or short (specify which)? Slender, medium, or stout (which)?
2. Color of eyes? Color of hair? Bald?
3. Has person lost arm, leg, hand, foot, or both eyes, or is he otherwise disabled (specify)?

The back was then signed by the registrar in response to this language: "I certify that my answers are true, that the person registered has read his own answers, that I have witnessed his signature, and that all of his answers of which I have knowledge are true, except as follows:" (followed by space to provide any registrar's comments). At the bottom of the back was the Precinct, City or County, State, and Date of registration.

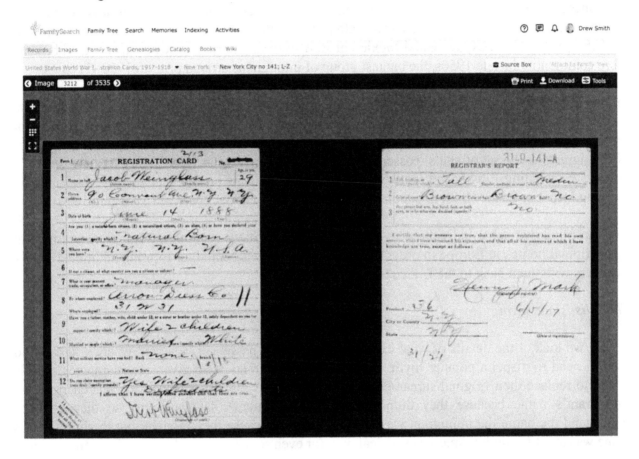

Figure 9.6: U.S. World War I Draft Registration Card for the author's great-uncle, Jacob Weinglass

For more information about military records from this time period

Neagles, James C. *U.S. Military Records: A Guide to Federal and State Sources, Colonial America to the Present*. Salt Lake City, Utah: Ancestry, 1994.

Immigration and Naturalization Records

Immigration

If you live in the United States, and you are not of 100% Native American ancestry, then you will have ancestors who emigrated to the United States or to a European colony in North America from elsewhere during genealogical time frames (after 1500). While some immigrants certainly came into the U.S. over land from Canada and Mexico or flew in from other countries once air travel became more common in the late 1950s, the biggest group of immigrants arrived prior to 1950 via ships.

Immigrants arriving via ship did so via many different U.S. port cities: Boston, Philadelphia, Baltimore, and New Orleans, just to name the more popular ones. But the most popular city for immigrant arrivals over all of U.S. history was New York City. And so the largest collection of records of immigrants is the set of ships' passenger lists for those arriving in New York City between 1820 and 1957, including Ellis Island (between 1892 and 1954) or its predecessor facility, the Emigrant Landing Depot at Castle Clinton, popularly known as Castle Garden (between 1855 and 1890).

Keep in mind that some individuals re-entered the United States multiple times, often returning to their original homes in Europe in order to support families left behind, or to bring additional family members with them back to the United States.

The Ellis Island myth

Before we look at the details of what can be found in these passenger lists, and where you can find them, I need to dispel a popular myth: the idea that immigrants were given new surnames at Ellis Island to replace their original surnames. The myth suggests that government officials changed the immigrant's name because they didn't speak the immigrant's language and so they couldn't understand the name the immigrant was telling them, or because they thought that the immigrant's name was too difficult for Americans to deal with (or even somehow "un-American"). None of this is true.

Certainly, some immigrants started to use a different surname at some point after they left their native country. However, what you will find on a ship's passenger list is the name they used when they bought their ticket for the journey, or the name that was added to the passenger list once they got onto the ship. When their ship arrived at Ellis Island, they were given a number pinned to their clothing, and that number corresponded to the entry on the ship's passenger list. In the Ellis Island facility, they were met by government officials who spoke a very wide range of European languages, and all that was needed was to find their name on the list and check them off.

Once they left Ellis Island, immigrants were free to use whatever surname they chose to, and some immigrants decided to change or simplify their surname in order to minimize discrimination or to better fit in. But this was their own choice, and not something done to them at Ellis Island. We may never know exactly why any immigrant's descendants heard a story of a forced surname change at Ellis Island, but there is no evidence that such a thing was even possible.

Information found on a ship's passenger list

As with other kinds of records, the amount of information provided on a ship's passenger list has evolved over time. For instance, a 21 March 1882 list showing the arrival of Anschel Grodowitz on the S.S. Bohemia from Hamburg has nothing more than his name, his age, his sex, his occupation, the country to which he belonged, and the country in which he intended to become an inhabitant. Later lists from the 1890s to the early 1920s might also indicate whether the immigrant could read and write and where they last lived.

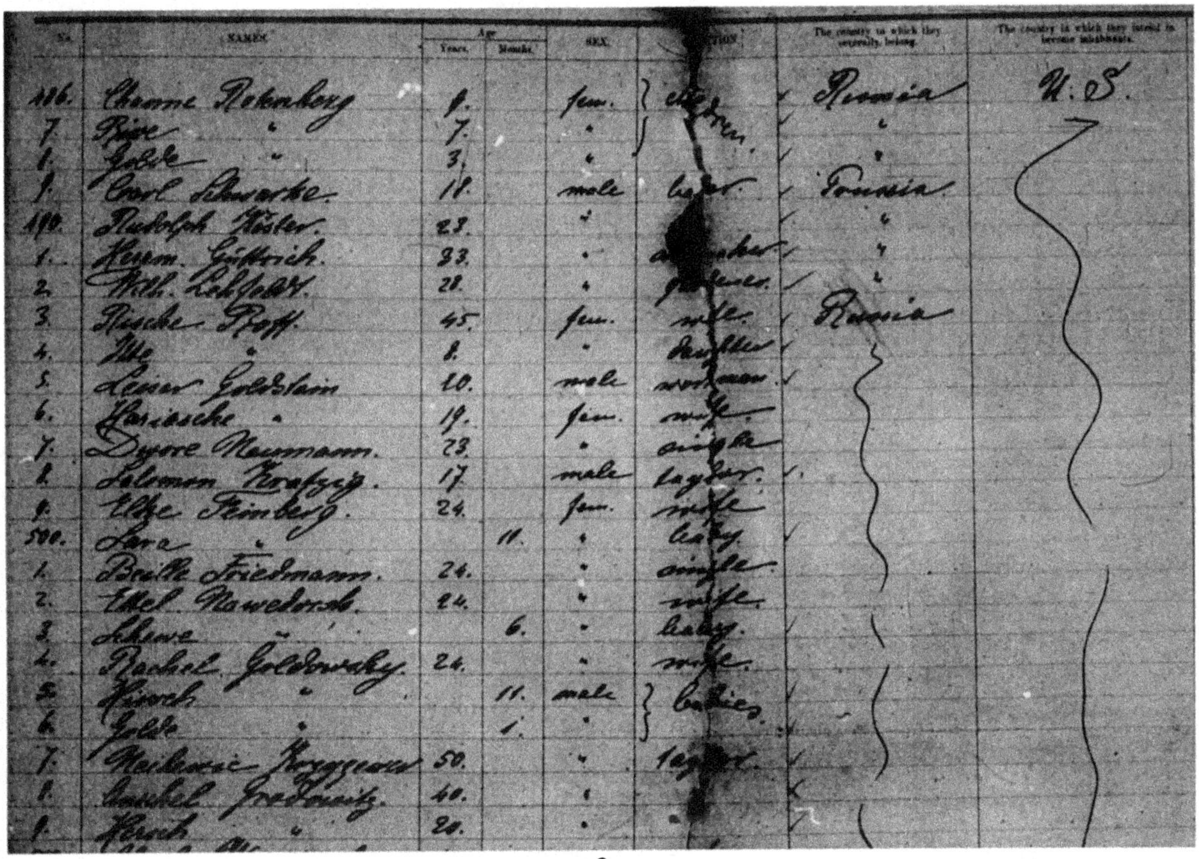

Figure 9.7: 1882 ship's passenger list for the S.S. Bohemia with an entry for the author's great-great-grandfather, Anschel Grodowitz

More recent lists, which might be typed instead of being handwritten, might be stretched across two pages and give additional information, such as marital status, the language that the immigrant could read, the city/town and country of birth, the name and address of a relative or friend back home, an indication of who paid for the passage, the name of a relative or friend and their address who they were going to join, health status, and a physical description (height, complexion, hair color, eye color, etc.).

Finding ship's passenger lists

FamilySearch provides access to this information in four separate collections:

- New York, New York Passenger and Crew Lists, 1909, 1925-1957
- New York Passenger Arrival Lists (Ellis Island), 1892-1924
- New York Passenger Lists, 1820-1891
- New York Book Indexes to Passenger Lists, 1906-1942

Ancestry.com provides a single searchable database for over 83 million individuals entitled: New York, U.S., Arriving Passenger and Crew Lists (including Castle Garden and Ellis Island), 1820-1957. MyHeritage provides a single searchable database of over 113 million individuals entitled: Ellis Island and Other New York Passenger Lists, 1820-1957. Findmypast provides a single searchable database of over 118 million individuals entitled: United States, Passenger and Crew Lists.

Naturalization

Naturalization is the legal process by which non-citizens can become citizens. In the United States, this provides naturalized citizens with a number of rights and benefits, including the right to vote, serve on a jury, and stand for public office, plus the freedom to travel outside the United States and return at any time. Many immigrants to the United States chose to go through the naturalization process after they arrived. Although naturalization laws have changed over time, the Naturalization Law of 1802 provided that:

- the alien needed to declare an intent to become a U.S. citizen at least 3 years in advance (known as "Declaration of Intent" or "First Papers")
- the alien needed to reside in the United States for at least 5 years
- the alien needed to complete the naturalization process through a petition to the local courts (known as "Second or Final Papers")
- children born outside the U.S. of naturalized citizens were to be considered citizens

Prior to September 1906, a woman was automatically naturalized if her husband naturalized, although she was not likely to be listed by name on her husband's naturalization paperwork. After September 1906 until 1922, she was listed by name. After 1922, a woman could naturalize separately from her husband. Because women in the United States didn't have the vote until the passage in 1920 of the 19th Amendment to the U.S. Constitution, women often didn't see any point in naturalization prior to that time.

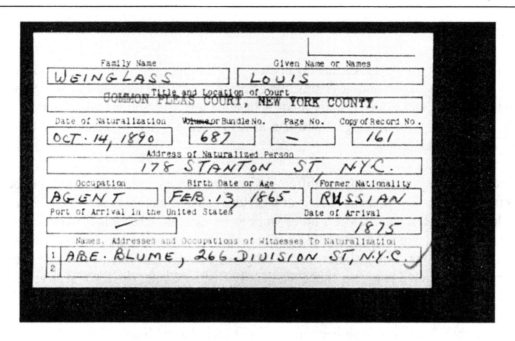

Figure 9.8: Naturalization card for Louis Weinglass, the author's great-grandfather

Finding naturalization records

Because immigrants could naturalize at federal, state, district, or local county courts, there is no one central repository for all U.S. naturalization records, and not all records have been digitized. In some cases, only the index cards for the original records have been digitized, in which case the actual record may need to be obtained directly from the relevant courthouse.

FamilySearch has 69 collections pertaining to naturalization, generally organized by state. In most cases, these records continue to be updated.

Ancestry has 141 collections for the United States in its "Citizenship Records" category. Nearly all of these are organized by state.

MyHeritage has 9 collections for the United States that include "Naturalization" as part of their titles. It provides free access to its largest collection of over 4 million records, entitled "U.S. Naturalization Records".

Findmypast has 14 collections for the United States that include "Naturalization" as part of their titles. The largest, "United States Naturalization Petitions", has over 8 million records.

For more information about immigration and naturalization

Quillen, W. Daniel. *Mastering Immigration & Naturalization Records* (3rd ed.). Cold Spring Press, 2015.

Church records

Apart from newspapers, cemeteries/funeral homes, and the publishers of city directories, religious institutions may be the largest non-governmental creators of personal records that are often accessible and useful for genealogists. For U.S. individuals with some sort of religious faith, Christian institutions will be the most common, although there has always been a small percentage of U.S. residents practicing non-Christian faiths.

Because records are kept differently by different Christian denominations (some at the local church level, others at a higher level), and because an individual church's records may have been lost if that church no longer exists, it can require a bit of work to locate church records for your own ancestors. Even if the records still exist, they may not have been digitized, or if digitized, they may be put online under certain restrictions. For instance, some religious records that have been made available to FamilySearch are restricted to access either at a Family History Center (FHC) or at an affiliated public library.

In some cases, church records have been indexed but included with other kinds of records, such as town records. As an example, Ancestry has a collection entitled Pennsylvania and New Jersey, U.S., Church and Town Records, 1669-2013, containing over 14 million records.

Churches often record events that are closely tied to related events recorded by government agencies. For instance, a government agency might record a birth, while a church might record an infant baptism and/or christening. The baptism/christening might occur immediately after birth or at least within a few days or weeks of the birth, although there are always exceptions. The government agency might record a marriage license and a marriage return, while the church might record the religious marriage ceremony. And the government agency might record a death, while the church might record the funeral service or burial.

As you search for church records about your ancestor, you will first need to identify what church your ancestor may have attended (or at least attended by close members of their family). You can then research how that church's denomination maintains its records: at the local level, or at a regional, state, or national level. I find it especially useful to go to the FamilySearch Catalog (familysearch.org/search/catalog) and do a search for records for a particular place (usually a city), then limit my search to "Church records". The FamilySearch Catalog will indicate which specific church each catalog entry refers to, and from there, you can figure out where the records might be.

Let's use my paternal grandfather's church as an example. The Smith family was Catholic and lived in Newark, New Jersey, since the early 1840s when they first arrived from Ireland. Their church was St. James, a Catholic Church that had primarily Irish-American members.

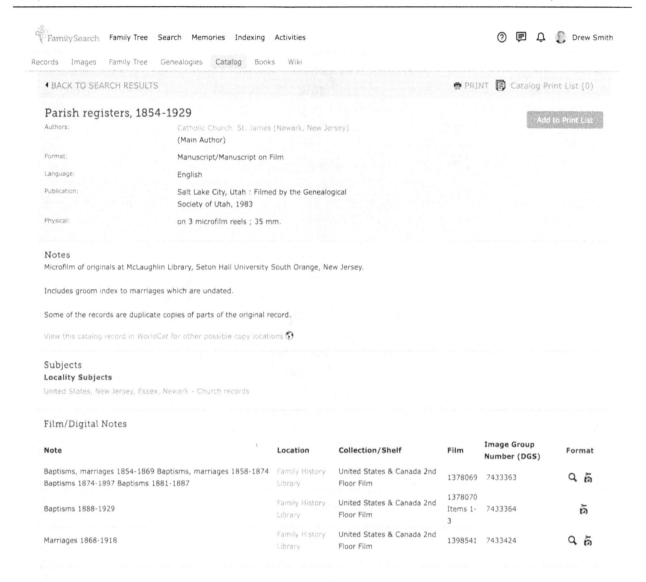

Figure 9.9: FamilySearch entry for records from St. James Catholic Church in Newark, New Jersey

For more information about church records

Morton, Sunny Jane, and Harold A. Henderson. *How to Find Your Family History in U.S. Church Records*. Baltimore: Genealogical Pub. Co., 2019.

Probate records

Probate is the legal process by which a deceased person's last will and testament is validated and their estate is managed for the purposes of distribution to the deceased person's heirs. Probate records include not only the person's will but also the papers associated with evaluating the estate and determining exactly how it will be distributed, and to whom.

I have waited until the end of this chapter to address probate records for several reasons: First, they are only recently becoming digitized and being placed online, but the vast majority of these are still available only on paper and must be consulted at the county courthouse where they were filed, and second, even the online versions may not have been indexed, requiring a lot of viewing of images in order to find the right ones.

Not everyone had a will. Those who died without making a will are said to have died *intestate*. Even in such cases, the probate court may have a little bit of paperwork to indicate that no will was found and that the estate was administrated and distributed appropriately, according to state laws.

If a person had a will, they usually designated at least one other individual (such as one of their adult children, an adult children's spouse, another relative, or a close friend) to be in charge of making sure that the provisions of the will were carried out according to instructions. This designated individual was the *executor*. This person (or a close relative if the deceased died intestate) would then go to the courts in order to obtain a *letter of administration*, a legal document allowing them to manage the estate and deal with its distribution. In some cases, the estate may have been managed by an administrator or a guardian.

Because probate is handled at the county level and not at the federal or state level, you'll need to begin by identifying the U.S. county where the deceased is most likely to have filed their will, generally where they regularly resided at the time of their death (which is not necessarily where they died). You can then use the FamilySearch Research Wiki to see where the probate records for a given county are kept. The Wiki will tell you if the records have been digitized (and if so, where they are to be found online), or what the address of the courthouse is if you are going to have to visit there yourself or have someone do it on your behalf.

Although probate records are kept at the county level, some online repositories, such as FamilySearch, have pulled together all the records for a given state in order to create a single collection that you can search.

As you look for collections of probate records, you'll encounter the terms *bound volumes* and *loose papers*. While these terms obviously refer to the format in which the records were filed, they also suggest that the types of information found in the different formats will differ. The bound volumes consist of the most important paperwork related to the probate process, especially the will itself. These bound volumes may begin with a roughly alphabetical index of names found later in the volume, or the index to a lot of volumes may be found in a separate volume. Other paperwork, such as the inventory of the estate and the sale of the estate property may be found in the bound volumes or may be found in the loose papers. Regardless, you'll want to search through both formats of documentation when learning about your ancestor's property and its distribution.

For example, the index to the estates for Newberry County, South Carolina, has been published and covers the years 1785 to 1949. It has been digitized and is online at FamilySearch. A master index appears at the top of every page indicating where the first two letters of the surname can be found. For instance, "Bo" is found beginning on page 31. I can use that to quickly find an entry for my great-grandmother's nephew, Josiah Walter Bodie Sr., which tells me that the estate was filed in 1926, that his son Albert B. Bodie was the administrator, and that the material is filed in package 591 and box 228. This information would allow me to locate the paperwork associated with this estate.

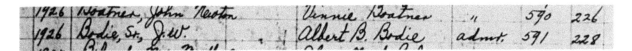

Figure 9.10: FamilySearch estates index for records from Newberry County, South Carolina

For more information about probate records

Rose, Christine. *Courthouse Research for Family Historians: Your Guide to Genealogical Treasures* (2nd ed.). CR Publishing, 2020.

Smith, Kenneth L. *Estate Inventories: How to Use Them*. Masthof Press, 2000.

Chapter 10:
Generations from 1850 to 1880 in the U.S.

As you move back in time before the 1880 census, you'll continue to work with records that you've already learned about. Newspapers, vital records, immigration and naturalization records, church records, and probate records will still be of value, although most U.S. states did not record vital records at the state level prior to 1880. Instead, you'll be looking for vital records, if they exist at all, at the county or town level.

In this chapter, we'll focus on the U.S. federal censuses (1850, 1860, and 1870), which you will discover have some major differences from later censuses. We'll look at the related 1850 and 1860 slave schedules. We'll be dealing with military records related to the major American conflict of that period, the U.S. Civil War. Finally, we'll discover the Freedmen's Bureau records, which were created in the immediate aftermath of the Civil War for the benefit of the enslaved people who were now free.

The U.S. Federal Censuses (1870, 1860, and 1850)

You've already been introduced to the concept of the U.S. federal census, taken every year since 1790. Over time, more and more questions were added, and we are somewhat spoiled with the censuses beginning in 1880 because they tell us exactly how all the members of the household are related to the head of the household and the marital status of each person. Unfortunately, as you go back to 1870 and earlier, we lose that important piece of information.

It is tempting to assume that a household headed by an adult male and including an adult woman of approximately the same age and with the same surname are husband and wife, and that any children listed are their children. However, it cannot be ruled out that the two adults are brother and sister or that the children are nieces and nephews. So while we can make some reasonable assumptions, we cannot know with any certainty the exact relationships without finding other sources of information (such as vital, church, and probate records).

Information in the 1870 census includes name, age, sex, color, occupation, and the value of any real estate and any personal estate. We can learn where the person was born (the U.S. state, U.S. territory, or other country). The 1870 census asks whether the parents were foreign born, the month in the past year if the person was born or married during that month, whether or not the person attended school in the past year, whether or not the person can read and write, whether the person has any special conditions (physical or mental issues, pauper, convict, etc.), and finally whether or not the person is an adult male citizen and whether or not the adult male citizen has lost his right to vote for some reason.

The 1860 census is simpler, telling us name, age, sex, color, occupation, value of real/personal estate, place of birth, whether married or attended school in the past year, whether they are adults who can't read or write, and whether they have those special conditions (as in the 1870). The 1850 census is almost exactly like the 1860 but asks only about real estate (not personal estate).

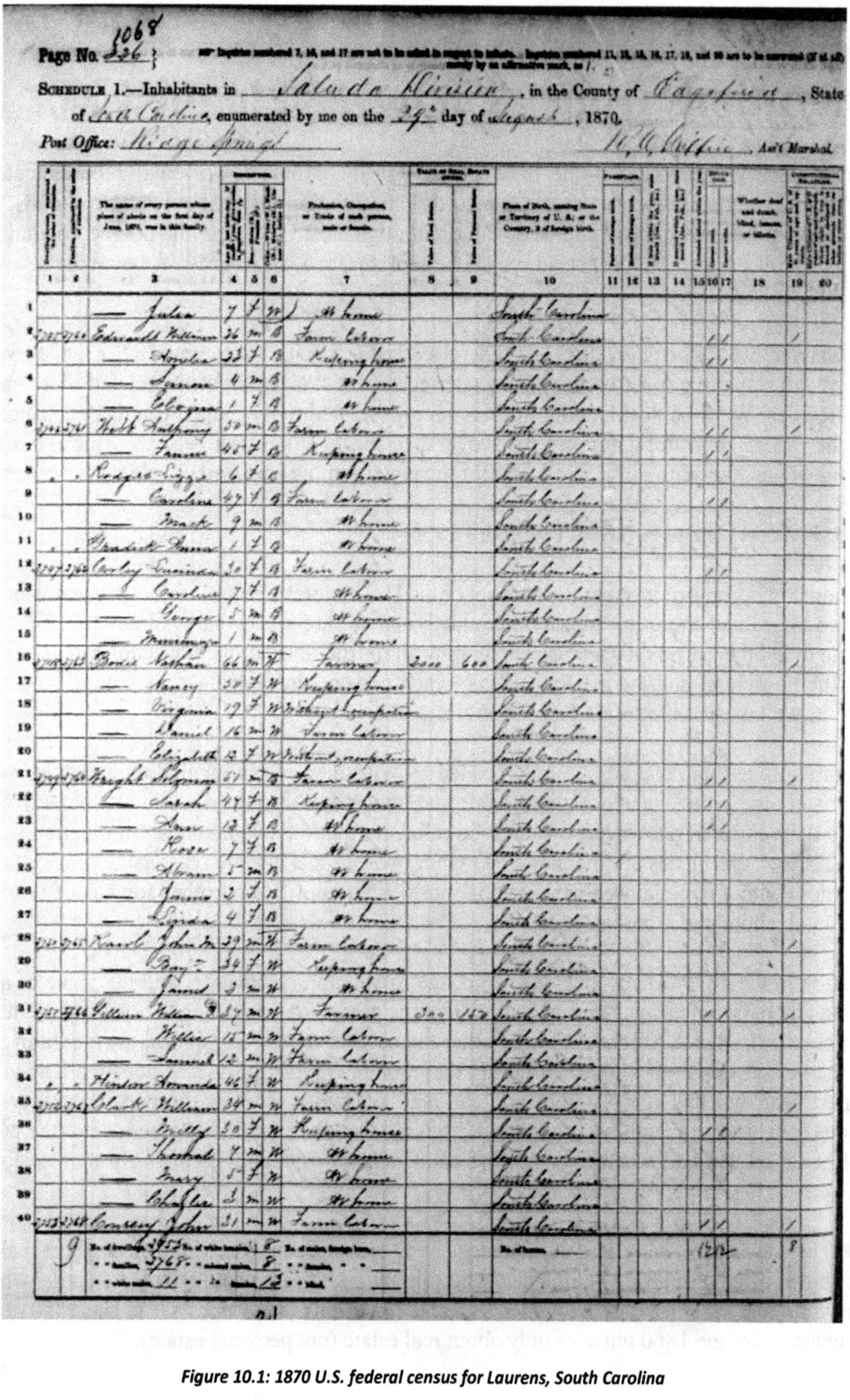

Figure 10.1: 1870 U.S. federal census for Laurens, South Carolina

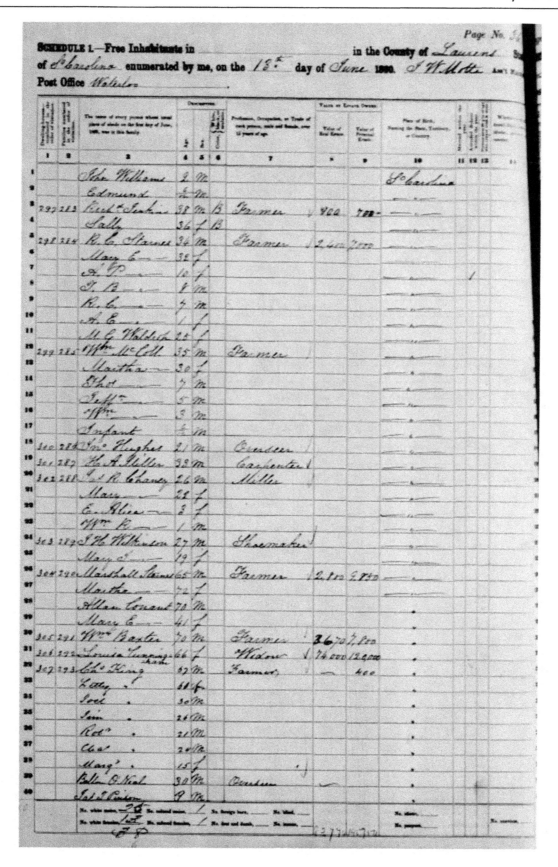

Figure 10.2: 1860 U.S. federal census for Laurens, South Carolina

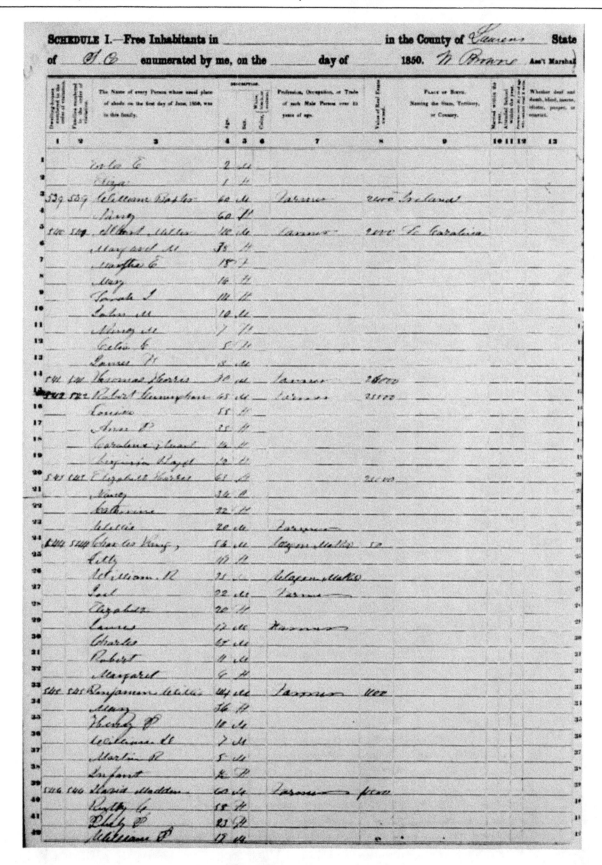

Figure 10.3: 1850 U.S. federal census for Laurens, South Carolina

Slave schedules (1850 and 1860)

Apart from probate records, the most detailed records we have for enslaved people in the United States prior to the Civil War are the 1850 and 1860 slave schedules. States and territories included in both of these schedules were Alabama, Arkansas, Delaware, District of Columbia, Florida, Georgia, Kentucky, Louisiana, Maryland, Mississippi, Missouri, North Carolina, South Carolina, Tennessee, Texas, Utah Territory, Virginia, plus New Jersey in 1850.

Unfortunately, slave schedules rarely tell us the names of the enslaved individuals. Instead, they tell us only the name of the enslaver, the number of enslaved individuals, and their age, sex, and color. They indicate if the individual was considered a fugitive from a state, whether the individual had been freed (manumitted), and whether the individual had physical (hearing or vision) problems or mental issues. The 1860 slave schedule also asked for the number of slave houses.

Information from slave schedules can lead to probate records that may provide additional information about the enslaved individuals, including their names and other details.

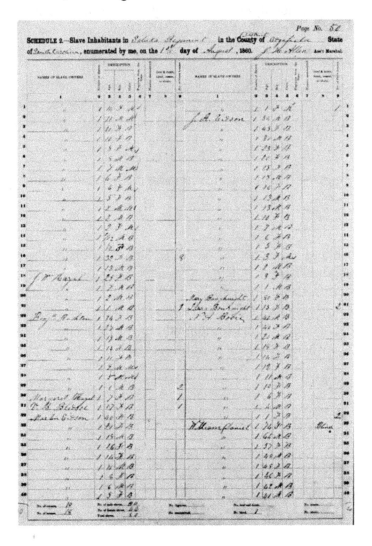

Figure 10.4: 1860 slave schedule for Edgefield District, South Carolina

Records from the U.S. Civil War

Between 1861 and 1865, the military conflict between the United States Army (popularly known as the Union Army) and the Confederate States Army (popularly known as the Confederate Army) generated a large number of records. After the Civil War ended, additional records were created regarding the combatants' military pensions, both for the individual who fought and for some members of their families (especially mothers and widows).

In addition to records concerning the specific individuals who fought, there may be additional records for the military units that they were part of, including names of those who led the units, the locations that they were assigned to, and the battles in which the units fought. These unit histories can provide useful information about your ancestor's military service during the Civil War.

Begin your research into your ancestor's military history by identifying whether he was of the appropriate age to have fought, keeping in mind that individuals who were normally too young or too old may still have participated, in some cases lying about their age to allow their participation. The 1860 census can be helpful in identifying the age of your ancestor and his location, which can be useful when looking for the right regiment and company. (Newspapers may also shed light on which individuals were joining which military units.)

Many military records regarding the U.S. Civil War can be found at FamilySearch, Ancestry, and the National Archives and Records Administration (NARA). Many other records are also kept at Fold3, a separate online repository operated by Ancestry. Your local public library may subscribe to Fold3 Library Edition.

At this point, let's focus on two kinds of records: service records and pension records.

Service records

Based on family information, I knew that the only direct ancestor I had who participated in the Civil War was my great-grandfather, Robert B. King, a resident of Laurens County, South Carolina. Using records from a number of different sources, including the South Carolina Department of Archives and History, I learned that King was part of Captain Jeter's Company, Macbeth Light Artillery, a part of the South Carolina Light Artillery. Fold3 has digital images of his service records, constituting 17 pages. These pages tell me when and where he enlisted, and how long he served.

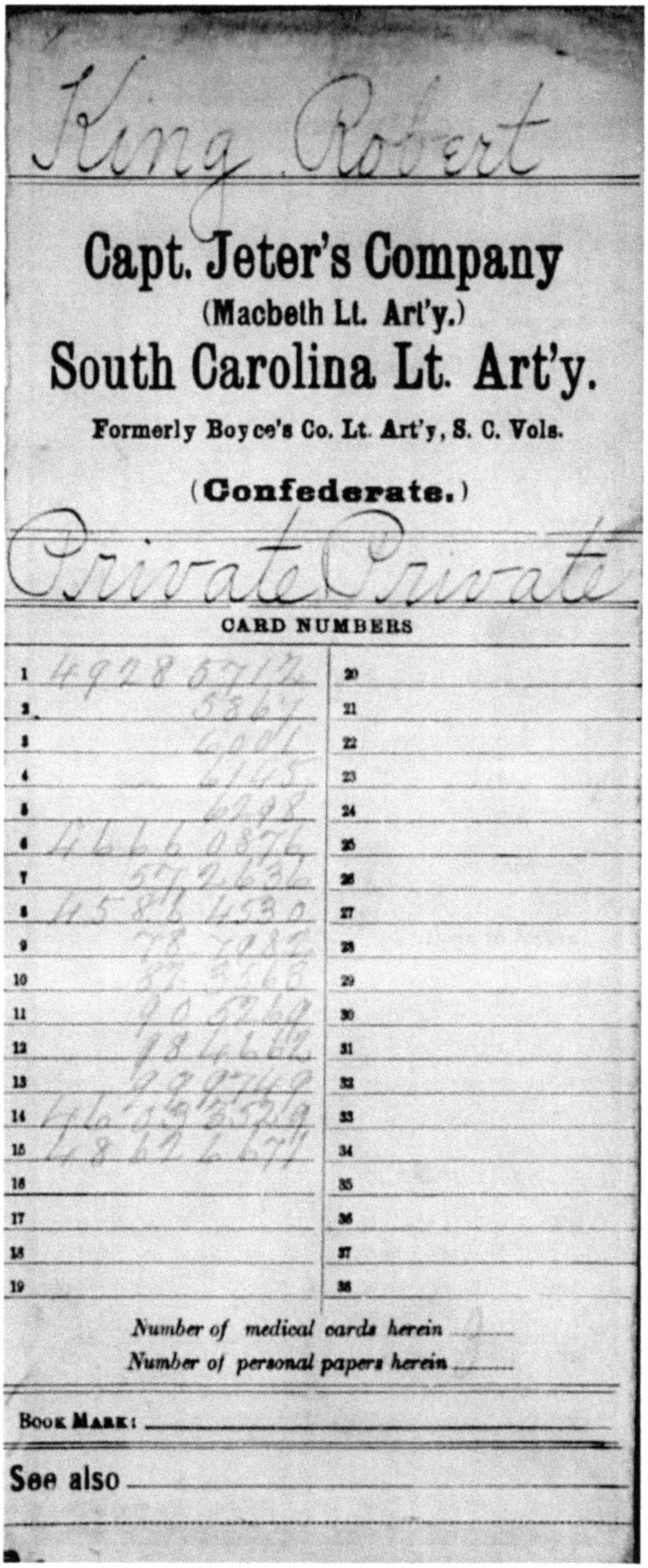

Figure 10.5: Index to the Confederate Army service record of Robert King, the author's great-grandfather

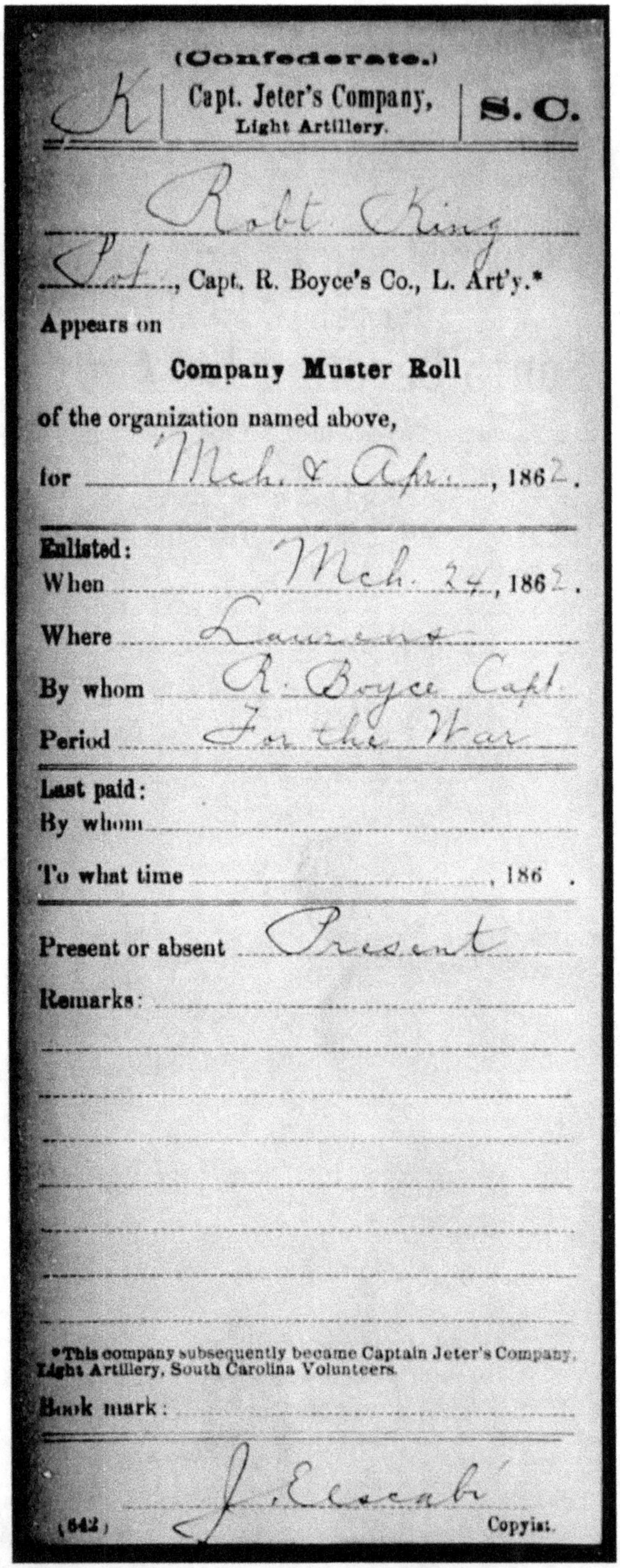

(Confederate.)

K | Capt. Jeter's Company, Light Artillery. | S. C.

Robt King

Pvt, Capt. R. Boyce's Co., L. Art'y.*

Appears on

Company Muster Roll

of the organization named above,

for Mch. & Apr., 1862.

Enlisted:

When Mch. 24, 1862.

Where Laurens

By whom R. Boyce Capt

Period For the War

Last paid:

By whom

To what time , 186 .

Present or absent Present

Remarks:

*This company subsequently became Captain Jeter's Company, Light Artillery, South Carolina Volunteers.

Book mark:

J. Escab

(642) Copyist.

Figure 10.6: Company muster roll entry for Robert King, the author's great-grandfather

Pension records

Pension records for Union soldiers are maintained by NARA, while those for Confederate soldiers are usually found in state archives. In some cases, the records have been digitized and placed online.

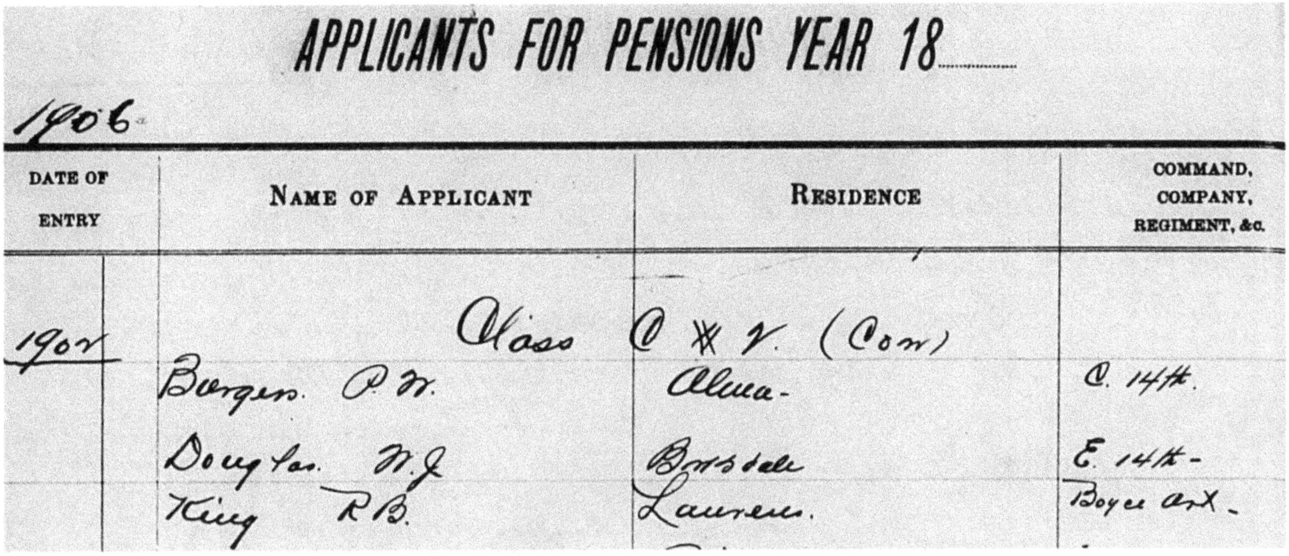

APPLICANTS FOR PENSIONS YEAR 18

1906

DATE OF ENTRY	NAME OF APPLICANT	RESIDENCE	COMMAND, COMPANY, REGIMENT, &c.
1907	Class	C W V. (Con)	
	Burgess P. W.	Allen-	C. 14th.
	Douglas W. J	Barksdale	E. 14th-
	King R.B.	Laurens.	Boyce Art.

Figure 10.7: Pension applicant list showing the name of R.B. King, the author's great-grandfather

Freedmen's Bureau

The U.S. government recognized that the sudden freeing of four million enslaved people at the end of the Civil War would result in an immediate and overwhelming need for employment, food, clothing, shelter, education, medical support, and banking. As a result, the Bureau of Refugees, Freedmen, and Abandoned Lands (popularly known as the Freedmen's Bureau) was established in 1865. Expected to last only one year, the Bureau continued to operate in some form until being dismantled in 1872. The records generated by the Freedmen's Bureau are enormously beneficial to those African-American genealogists with previously enslaved ancestors, as well as to other genealogists whose ancestors were employed by the Freedmen's Bureau.

Although FamilySearch has long had digitized images of Freedmen's Bureau records, only a portion of those were indexed and in many cases were kept separated by state. In 2021, Ancestry released a single comprehensive and indexed collection of nearly three million Freedmen's Bureau records. These records may make it possible to link formerly enslaved ancestors to particular plantations or to individual enslavers, and then to use that information to further identify enslaved individuals in wills, probate, and property records.

States included in the Ancestry collection are Alabama, Arkansas, Delaware, District of Columbia, Florida, Georgia, Kentucky, Louisiana, Maryland, Mississippi, Missouri, North Carolina, South Carolina, Tennessee, Texas, and Virginia.

Records found in the Freedmen's Bureau collections include employment, ration lists, school records, hospital records, and banking records. There are also pension records, court documents, and tax assessments. All these documents may name formerly enslaved individuals and identify where they were living and working. Those with European ancestry may have ancestors who were employed by the Freedmen's Bureau or who participated in the operation of its schools and hospitals.

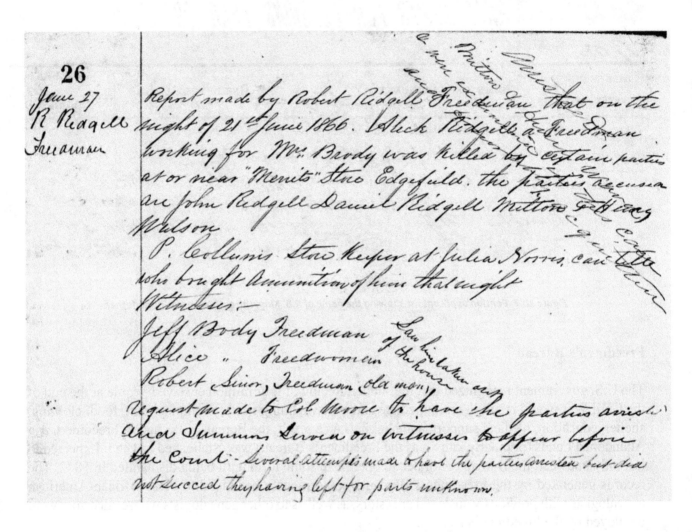

Figure 10.8: Example of court record from the Freedmen's Bureau

Chapter 11:
Generations from 1776 to 1850 in the U.S.

Learning about your ancestors before 1850 in the United States is going to be more difficult than later periods, especially for two reasons: one, the older a record is, the less likely that it has been preserved and survived to the present day; and two, older records of a given type generally provide less detail than later ones. For instance, some of the earliest census records were lost due to the British attack on Washington, DC, during the War of 1812. Of course, there are always exceptions, but we'll need to set our expectations appropriately.

You'll continue to use newspapers, vital records, immigration and naturalization records, church records, and probate records. We'll certainly be looking at census records and military records, and we go into detail on that in this chapter.

Historical maps may become critical for researching in this time period because so many places of the period may no longer exist or may have changed names. Speaking of maps, we'll introduce land and property records in this chapter, although you will find much of this information useful for later time periods, too.

The U.S. Federal Census (1790 to 1840)

If you thought that it was disappointing in the 1850-1870 censuses to lose the relationship information, be prepared for the pre-1850 censuses. The earliest U.S. censuses are challenging because they name only the head of the household (usually an adult male) and provide no names for anyone else. Instead, they use tick marks or numbers in a number of different columns to indicate how many males and how many females there were, and in what age groups.

Given that the original purpose of the census was simply to count how many people lived in each geographic area so that congressional representation could be fairly appointed, very little other information was of interest to the U.S. government. However, age ranges, especially for males, was certainly of some interest as it indicated to the U.S. government how many men could be called up if an army was needed.

Before we get into tips on how to get the most from these early censuses, let's look at the specific information provided by each census.

1790

The census schedules for a number of states were lost. The missing states include Delaware, Georgia, Kentucky, New Jersey, Tennessee, and Virginia.

- Name of head of family
- Number of free white males 16 or over
- Number of free white males under 16

- Number of free white females
- Number of other free people (people of color, including taxed Native Americans)
- Number of slaves

1800

The census schedules for a number of states and territories were lost. The missing areas include Georgia, Indiana Territory, Kentucky, Mississippi Territory, New Jersey, Northwest Territory, Tennessee, Virginia, and the Alexandria County portion of the District of Columbia.

Same information as for 1790, but age columns for free white males and free white females are broken down into: Under 10, 10-15, 16-25, 26-44, 45 & Over.

1810

The census schedules for a number of states and territories were lost. The missing areas include the District of Columbia, Georgia, Indiana Territory, Louisiana Territory (Missouri), Mississippi Territory, New Jersey, and Tennessee. Illinois Territory's St. Clair County was lost, as were all counties for Ohio except for Washington County.

Same information as for 1800.

1820

The census schedules for a number of states and territories were lost. The missing areas include Arkansas Territory, Missouri Territory, New Jersey, as well as a number of counties in Alabama, North Carolina, and Tennessee.

Same information as for 1810, but with the addition of:

- Number of foreigners who have not yet naturalized
- Number of persons engaged in agriculture
- Number of persons engaged in commerce
- Number of persons engaged in manufactures
- Age and sex breakdown for slaves and separately for free colored persons: To 14, 14-25, 26-44, 45 & up
- All other persons except those Native Americans not taxed

Note: The 1820 census also adds a column not appearing in any other census: a separate column counting those 16 to 18. This means that those in this age range will be counted twice (they are also counted in the 16 to 25 column), but this enumeration gave extra information to the U.S. government regarding how many men would be available for military service.

1830

The census schedules exist for all states, but some counties are missing for Maryland, Massachusetts, and Mississippi.

Age ranges for free white persons are now divided into: Under 5, 5-10, 10-15, 15-20, 20-30, 30-40, 40-50, 50-60, 60-70, 70-80, 80-90, 90-100, and over 100. Age ranges for slaves and for freed colored persons are now divided into: Under 10, 10-24, 24-36, 36-55, 55-100, and over 100.

In addition to counting the number of foreigners (white persons only) who have not yet naturalized, this census also counts (separately for white persons and for slaves/colored persons) the number of individuals who are deaf (divided into Under 14, 14-25, and 25 & up) or who are blind.

1840

The census schedules exist for all states.

Same information as for 1830.

Tips for using the pre-1850 censuses

If all you have are numbers and no names prior to 1850, how can you use these censuses? Begin by making sure you have as much information as you can from later censuses, especially the 1850 census, including genders and ages. Use those to match up against the numbers appearing in earlier censuses. You may want to create a timeline for each individual to see how old they would be in each earlier census.

A spreadsheet can be helpful for these censuses. By aligning these censuses with each census being a row, you can watch as unnamed individuals move from column to column as they age, providing you with clues as to their exact ages.

To put names to the unnamed individuals in the earlier censuses, you'll need to look to all of the other record types (newspapers, vital records, church records, and probate records).

Military Records (the Revolutionary War and the War of 1812)

Just as our later genealogical research periods were marked by military activity, the same is certainly true for the U.S. period before 1850, especially due to the Revolutionary War and the War of 1812. Approximately 231,000 men served in the Revolutionary War's Continental Army, and nearly 500,000 men served during the War of 1812, most for local defense purposes.

The best sources for military records from this period can be found on Ancestry's Fold3 service, which is available via personal subscription but which may also be a subscription that your local public library provides. Even without Fold3, both FamilySearch and Ancestry have significant military collections for the 1700's and early 1800's. In addition, you will want to check with the appropriate state archive to see what military records they may have.

United States Revolutionary War Rolls, 1775-1783

This collection of approximately 1.5 million records, created from documents stored at the National Archives and found on both FamilySearch and Ancestry, provides access to muster rolls and other types of military records.

United States Revolutionary War Pension and Bounty Land Warrant Applications, 1800-1900

Many veterans later claimed pensions for their military service, normally in cases where the veteran was disabled and unable to provide a living for himself and his family. A veteran's widow may also have applied for a pension. Pension applications are a rich source of genealogical information, not only about the veteran himself but also about his family. For instance, his widow may have had to provide documentation to prove her marriage to the deceased veteran. (I've heard of cases where a woman ripped pages out of her family bible and submitted them as part of the application in order to prove her marriage to the veteran.) Not all pension applications were approved, and some were set aside until more documentation could be provided. These pension files could be very brief (even just a single card) or dozens of pages long.

The U.S. Federal Government, in order to reward the veterans or their heirs, granted free land to them, known as *bounty land*. As with pensions, veterans (or their heirs) could apply for bounty land and may have been rewarded with some number of acres. While you may think of the term *patent* as referring only to something granted to an inventor, the term is also used to refer to a grant of land by the government (specifically referred to as a *land patent*).

Your own ancestors may have applied for a pension or for bounty land on behalf of themselves, or their widow or heirs may have done so. Or your ancestors' names may appear on affidavits that were submitted as part of applications for someone else, perhaps to attest to the applicant's service record, to his disability, or to his marriage.

The United States Revolutionary War Pension and Bounty Land Warrant Applications, 1800-1900 is a collection that can be found on Fold3, but the index to it is also located on FamilySearch.

War of 1812

Records from FamilySearch that can be useful for those who served in the War of 1812 include:

- United States War of 1812 Index to Service Records, 1812-1815
- United States Registers of Enlistments in the U.S. Army, 1798-1914
- United States Muster Rolls of the Marine Corps, 1798-1937
- United States, War of 1812 Index to Pension Application Files, 1812-1910

Records from Ancestry:

- U.S., War Bounty Land Warrants, 1789-1858

Land and property records

We'll do an introduction here, but for more information on this topic, go to Margaret Law Hatcher's 2014 book *Locating Your Roots: Discover Your Ancestors Using Land Records.*

While it's true that you would want to look at land and property records for your ancestors in later time periods, they are especially critical for the pre-1850 periods when other records may be hard to find. We would already have seen references to land and other property in probate records, when property was passed down to heirs (and sometimes subdivided among multiple heirs). As you might imagine, most land and property records can be found at local county courthouses, and so may not have yet been digitized and made available online.

When European colonialism began in North America, the settlers and their governments came into conflict with local indigenous peoples, sometimes resulting in treaties requiring that the indigenous people cede their land to the European governments. The earliest lands that were granted to settlers in British America used a *metes and bounds* system to describe the boundaries of each owner's piece of land. These boundaries could be described using watercourses (creeks, rivers, etc.), walls, buildings, and roads, and might use landmarks such as trees, rocks, or stone markers to describe the ends of the boundaries. Boundaries might also be described in terms of compass directions and distances. The land descriptions might also refer to the names of who owned the adjoining pieces of land. As you might imagine, the problem with this system is that trees, rocks, buildings, and walls could disappear, and watercourses could alter their banks.

Once the new United States government signed the Treaty of Paris with the British government, granting the land west of the Appalachian Mountains all the way to the Mississippi River, a better system (the *public lands* system) was created to mark land boundaries that would end up in the hands of westward-moving settlers. The Public Land Survey System (PLSS) uses meridians (north-south lines) and baselines (east-west lines) to act as starting points for locating property, and then subdivides land into large rectangular areas that can be divided into smaller pieces. You may run into the term *township* (short for *surveyor township*) as an area of 36 square miles that can be divided into 36 *sections* of one square mile. These sections are then subdivided into quarters (160 acres), and each quarter into quarter-quarters (40 acres).

You can see that, depending on where in the United States your ancestors owned land, you will need to learn which system (metes and bounds vs. public lands) was used to identify its boundaries. Historical maps will be essential to get a good understanding of where your ancestors' land was.

Although for the vast majority of cases, you'll need to visit the appropriate county courthouse to view indexes and then the records themselves for the description and sale of land, the public lands *tract books* can be searched or browsed on FamilySearch as part of the United States Bureau of Land Management Tract Books, 1800-c. 1955.

...ore 1776

12:

...erations in British America before 1776

In this chapter we'll be talking about British America prior to the American Revolutionary War, and specifically about the Thirteen Colonies. Although my father's ancestors didn't arrive in the northern United States from Ireland and Poland until the mid-to-late 1800s, my mother's ancestors were Southerners, some of whom were almost certainly in British America prior to 1776. At least one of my ancestral lines, the Boddies, appear to have been present in Virginia since the mid-1600s.

Where do we look for records, especially in this time period prior to any U.S. federal census? Although some of the relevant records would be in the hands of The National Archives (TNA) of the United Kingdom in London, where could you find records still existing either online or in the hands of state and local archives? Yes, if you're an American researcher with colonial roots, you could travel to TNA and do research there, but beginning genealogists would be better served by starting with records closer to home.

Let's remind ourselves of the types of resources that we've already used, which can still provide rich genealogical information about our colonial ancestors. Newspapers, cemeteries, military records, church records, probate records, and land/property records are going to continue to be important sources. Once we get back to colonial times, we may find that other researchers have already done a lot of the heavy lifting, and published books and articles or left their papers to archives (see Chapter 5 about this).

Now let's look at some record types and locations that we haven't spent much time on yet.

State archives

If there is one place that is most likely to house records of the Thirteen Colonies, it is the archives for the states that those colonies eventually became. While some of this material may have been digitized and placed online (often by the state archive itself on its own website), you may also need to travel to the state archive to do research or ask someone who lives closer to do it on your behalf.

Obviously, each state archive is going to differ from others in what it contains and what it provides online. For example, if I were doing research in North Carolina, I would visit the website for the State Archives of North Carolina (archives.ncdcr.gov). The menu choice for Search Catalog leads to their Discover Online Catalog (DOC) and a link to Search DOC. I'll look for a relative who lived in North Carolina in colonial times. A search for Nathan Boddie gives 14 results, including a number of land records from 1761-1762 (see Figure 12.1). This information can be used to either request the information, or to have someone (myself or a friend) visit to obtain the information.

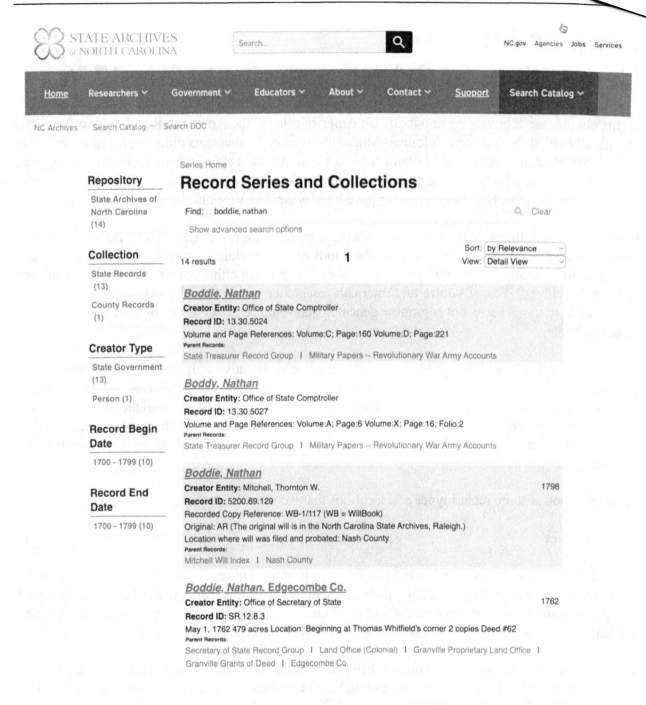

Figure 12.1: Records concerning Nathan Boddie from the State Archives of North Carolina

Vital records (town level)

We have previously looked at vital records (Chapter 8) kept at the state level, but if you need the earliest available vital records, you'll need to look for county or town records. Unfortunately for those with ancestors from other parts of the United States, these records are generally limited to New England and New York. In some cases, these have been made available at a state archive or microfilmed by FamilySearch. For the FamilySearch materials, you may be able to view the images online from home, or you may need to visit a local Family History Center or affiliated public library to see them.

Another good source for early New England or New York records is American Ancestors, a website from the New England Historic Genealogical Society. Their online collections contain over 1.4 billion searchable names.

Tax records

An early 18th-century proverb tells us that nothing is certain but death and taxes. When it comes to records, we may find it very difficult to find early death records, but we can often find tax records. For thousands of years, governments have taxed their citizens (as well as non-citizen residents), and the British and U.S. governments are no exceptions. We could certainly have covered tax records in earlier chapters, but because we had other records, such as census records, tax records were of somewhat lower priority. Because tax rolls are often compiled every year, they can certainly fill in gaps between the decennial years of a census. But let's now look at how tax records can help us with research in the time of the Thirteen Colonies.

Because the laws of colonial times normally limited property ownership to adult males, you'll usually find only property-owning adult males named in colonial tax documents. While it is certainly possible for a man to own property in one jurisdiction while living elsewhere, tax rolls can often provide an idea of where families were living at given times. They can point us to courthouses where we can then look for land records and probate records.

As with any other type of record from these very early time periods, we cannot assume that the tax records have survived to the present day. The vast majority of these records have not yet been digitized or placed online, but you can still look for them in the usual places, including FamilySearch, Ancestry, and American Ancestors. State archives and state historical societies may also have copies, or copies may exist at the county or town level. For instance, there are four rolls of microfilm from the Massachusetts state archives for valuations and tax documents from the 1760s that can be viewed online at a nearby Family History Center or affiliated public library.

In addition to tax records, the same repositories may also hold related types of records, such as court order books and tithe lists. Check with the repository to see what types of records they might have for the geographical area your ancestor was from. Genealogical.com (the publisher of this book) has an extensive collection of 17th- and 18th-century compiled source records and genealogical compendia that are available in digital subscription format, as well as in print.

Chapter 13:
Generations Outside the U.S. (in English)

This book was created with the U.S-based beginner researcher in mind, with an assumption that one or more ancestral lines were present in the United States and possibly back to the Thirteen Colonies of British America. But at some point, unless your ancestry is 100% Native American, at least some of your ancestors came to North America from other places in genealogical timeframes. In this chapter, we'll look primarily at how to begin looking for ancestors from Canada (English-speaking parts), the United Kingdom, or Ireland. (The next chapter will get into using records that weren't recorded in English or researching ancestry from places where English was not the language of record-keeping.)

Canada (English)

Many Americans can trace their ancestry back to people who were living in the English-speaking parts of Canada. My Aunt Cleo's second husband was from Canada, so I'll be using him in examples in this section.

You'll find the major online repositories (FamilySearch, Ancestry, and MyHeritage, among others) especially useful for Canadian research. And just as the United States has NARA and the Library of Congress, Canada has Library and Archives Canada (available in both English and French, at bac-lac.gc.ca). You'll be wanting to explore what LAC has for genealogists.

Let's look at the most common records that will help with this Canadian research: newspapers, vital records, burial records, censuses, military records, church records, immigration/naturalization records, probate records, and land records.

Both Newspapers.com and NewspaperArchive have Canadian newspapers. MyHeritage provides access to nearly 7 million pages of Canadian newspapers, while Ancestry has Canadian marriage and obituary indexes to what is found on Newspapers.com. The University of Toronto Libraries has a research guide for Canadian newspapers, which can point you to things not found elsewhere. You'll find it at guides.library.utoronto.ca/newspapers/canada

Just as states have had the responsibility in the United States for civil registration of vital records (births, marriages, and deaths), that responsibility in Canada has fallen to the provinces. Depending on the province, these records may go back to the mid-1800s, or may be available only back to the early 1900s. Other vital records may be found associated with churches.

My aunt's second husband, Arthur Lamont McLeod, was born in 1907 in Canada and died in 1981 in San Diego. I have lots of American records that cover parts of his life, including his World War II draft card, his naturalization, and the record of his second marriage to my aunt. These records tell me that he was born on 17 August 1907 in Norwich, Canada, and that his parents' names were Angus McLeod and Annie Bond.

When I start looking for Canadian records, I can find Uncle Art's birth record in the Canada, Ontario Births, 1869-1912 collection. It confirms his birth date and location (the birth registration happened on September 11), that his mother's full name was Annie E. Bond, that the family was living on West Stover St., and that his father's occupation was as a Salvation Army Captain.

Burials in Canada can be found in many of the same online databases that were mentioned previously for the United States, such as Find a Grave and BillionGraves.

Canada has taken a national census every 10 years, on the years ending in 1. The Prairie Provinces (Alberta, Manitoba, and Saskatchewan) have also taken a census on the years ending in 6. Keep in mind that Newfoundland (today known as Newfoundland and Labrador) did not join the Canadian Confederation until 1949. Just as U.S. censuses are not released to the public until 72 years after it was taken, Canadian censuses are not available for 92 years. So at the time of this writing, the most recent available census is the 1921 Canada Census.

I can find Uncle Art in the 1911 Canadian census living with his parents and three siblings (Gordon, Grace, and Roy). The census provides lots of other details, including street address, month and year of birth, country of birth (or province if born in Canada), ethnicity (Uncle Art's father was Scottish), and religion.

Canadian historical military records cover the times from the mid-1700s until the early 1950s (the Korean War). Details on what is available (and where) can be found in a number of places, including Library and Archives Canada.

As mentioned previously, church records will be especially useful for vital records prior to when civil registration was kept. You'll have to first figure out what denomination your ancestors were affiliated with, and ideally, which specific church.

When individuals crossed from Canada to the United States between 1895 and 1954, those records were indexed as part of the St. Albans, Vermont, District, even when the crossing wasn't through the city of St. Albans. (Note that those heading from Europe to the United States may have first taken a ship to Halifax, Nova Scotia, or to Montreal, Quebec, and then taken a train to St. Albans, so this index is worth checking if you can't find your immigrant ancestors on a ship's passenger list for the United States.) The index is available on FamilySearch. I can find Uncle Art twice in the St. Albans records: the first time in 1908 when he is one year old, entering at Detroit with his mother, his older siblings, and his maternal grandparents; and the second time in 1914 entering at Detroit with his mother and siblings.

Ship's passenger lists are not likely to be found prior to 1865, but later records can be found at Library and Archives Canada, FamilySearch, and Ancestry. Naturalization for those arriving prior to 1867 would not have been needed if the immigrant was from England, Scotland, Wales, or Ireland. To find naturalization records, start with Library and Archives Canada.

The laws for probate for Canada (outside of Quebec) were similar to those for the United States. Pre-1930 probate records may now be at the provincial archives, while more recent records are with the particular court. Also check the FamilySearch catalog for the availability of pre-1930 probate records.

Finally, Canadian land records outside of Quebec share some similarities to U.S. land records. For instance, many of the pre-1870 records will look like the U.S. metes and bounds system (described in an earlier chapter), while the later records will resemble the U.S. public land system. You will want to start with looking for Ontario, Nova Scotia, and New Brunswick land records in the FamilySearch Catalog. Beyond that, you'll need to see what specific provincial land offices hold.

For more information about engaging in Canadian genealogical research, see the 2007 book *Finding Your Canadian Ancestors: A Beginners Guide* by Sherry Irvine and Dave Obee.

United Kingdom

Entire books have been written about how to conduct research into British ancestry, so we'll just go over the main points here.

Online repositories

While FamilySearch, Ancestry, and MyHeritage do contain British records, you may find that Findmypast, the London-based online genealogical repository, will provide you with the most records relevant to your British (or Irish) research.

The National Archives

The British equivalent of the U.S. NARA and the Canadian LAC is The National Archives (TNA), located in Kew on the western side of London. TNA (nationalarchives.gov.uk) focuses on records for England and Wales, as well as being the official repository for the government of the United Kingdom. As with other national archives, only a tiny percentage of all records have been digitized and placed online, but you'll want to visit the TNA website at nationalarchives.gov.uk to see what they might have for your own research.

Membership societies

Two large membership organizations can be of special help with your British research. The Society of Genealogists (sog.org.uk) not only has its own impressive library of British genealogical materials, but also has regular online educational sessions on various research topics. The Guild of One-Name Studies (one-name.org) focuses on the idea of researching everything that can be learned about those individuals carrying a specific surname (whether British or not) and assists its members with educational materials on how to do genealogical research. Both organizations send their members a well-produced periodical and will put you in touch with other researchers from around the world. I'm a proud member of both.

Newspapers

British newspapers can be found at both Newspapers.com and NewspaperArchive, but Findmypast partners with the British Library to provide an enormous collection of newspapers.

Vital records (births, marriages, and deaths)

As in the United States, you're most likely to find vital records using two types of sources: civil and religious. The biggest difference is that the civil records are not kept at a state level but instead are handled at a national level. These civil records officially began in England and Wales on 1 July 1837, although local compliance may have been hit-or-miss until new laws in 1874 (there were penalty fees for failing to register births in a timely manner, for example).

A good (and free) source for births, marriages, and deaths is the FreeUKGenealogy site (freeukgenealogy.org.uk). From their home page, you can click on "Search FreeBMD" and then search for your relatives among the 285 million records. You can view the image of the registers, which are done on a quarterly basis. Early records were handwritten, while later records were typed. For a birth record, you will get to see the district in which the birth was registered, together with a volume and page number. You may also get to see the mother's maiden name. The information provided in the registers can be used to order copies of the original records.

For births, marriages, and deaths after 1 July 1837, you will also want to look for religious records, and you will certainly need to use these for such events prior to 1 July 1837. These records may date back in some cases to the early 1500s, although you are more likely to find these in later years. The primary church of the time would be the Church of England (the Anglican Church). Other denominations, referred to as "Non-Conformist", also existed, so depending on the religious beliefs of your ancestors, you may need to look for Catholic or Protestant records as well. As in other countries, church records may include baptisms, marriages, and burials.

Burials

Burials in the United Kingdom can be found in Find a Grave, BillionGraves, and Interment.net.

Census records

The United Kingdom has also held a regular census every ten years, but unlike the United States, its census years are the years ending in 1. The censuses from 1801 to 1831 did not list people by name, so the genealogically useful censuses are those from 1841 to 1921. (Censuses are not released to the general public until 100 years after they are taken.) Censuses between 1841 and 1911 are available for free on FamilySearch, but are also available on the Ancestry and Findmypast subscription sites. The 1921 census was recently released but access is currently restricted to Findmypast (at an extra cost above regular Findmypast subscriptions) due to a partnership with The National Archives.

Scotland

Much of what has been previously described for the United Kingdom applies not only to England and Wales but also to Scotland, but there are also records that are specific to Scotland. To learn more about what may be available to you for Scottish research, visit the ScotlandsPeople website (scotlandspeople.gov.uk).

For more information about British research

There are numerous books that have been written in the last twenty years on the topic of British genealogical research. (Several include Irish research as well.) While there are countless books that focus on specific kinds of British records, the following three will provide you with a good general introduction to this research:

- *Quillen's Essentials of Genealogy: Tracing Your Irish & British Roots* by W. Daniel Quillen, published in 2012
- *Ancestral Trails: The Complete Guide to British Genealogy and Family History* (2nd ed.) by Mark D. Herber, published in 2006
- *In Search of Your British & Irish Roots: A Complete Guide to Tracing Your English, Welsh, Scottish, & Irish Ancestors* (4th ed.) by Angus Baxter, published in 2000

Ireland

Introduction

Many Americans have ancestry from the island of Ireland. Before we get into the complexity of where to find Irish records, it should be pointed out that the biggest problem faced by American researchers is knowing exactly where in Ireland their ancestors were from. Without that knowledge, it can be extremely difficult to pin down the correct ancestor, especially with common first names and common surnames.

To find the answer to the question of where in Ireland your ancestor was from, you'll need to use a wide range of American-based sources, including family stories, family papers, obituaries, gravestones, newspapers, and immigration records, just to name some of the most helpful. But be careful with many of these, as information can be confused as it passes from one generation to the next. In my own case, I'm fortunate enough to know the specific locations in Ireland for three of my four ancestral Irish lines due to Catholic Church marriage records in England and due to family letters that were preserved by a different branch of the family.

During most of the earliest times from which genealogical records still exist, Ireland was under control of England and then the United Kingdom. In 1922, the island of Ireland was officially split into the Irish Free State (later Ireland in 1937 and then the Republic of Ireland in 1948) and Northern Ireland, which remains part of the United Kingdom. Depending upon where in the island of Ireland your ancestors lived, you may need to use different archives and repositories.

Both for the Republic of Ireland and for Northern Ireland, you'll need to know what is kept at the national level and what is kept at the county level, especially the historical counties (boundaries may have changed a few times since 1974, but you'll generally be mostly interested in records from the time of the historical counties).

Archives and online repositories

The official government repositories are the National Archives (Republic of Ireland), online at nationalarchives.ie, and the Public Record Office of Northern Ireland (PRONI), online at nidirect.gov.uk/campaigns/public-record-office-northern-ireland-proni. You'll also want to see what is available for Irish research at FamilySearch, Ancestry, and Findmypast.

Newspapers

Look for Irish newspapers at Newspapers.com, NewspaperArchive, and Findmypast.

Vital records

To find birth, marriage, and death records, you'll look for the usual two types: civil registration and church records. Non-Catholic marriages were recorded as part of civil registration starting in 1845, but births, marriages (all religions), and deaths began registration in 1864. Church records may exist back to the 1700s for Protestant churches, and to 1829 for Catholic churches. Look for these records at irishgenealogy.ie (Republic of Ireland), the General Register Office Northern Ireland (GRONI), FamilySearch, and Findmypast.

Burials

The usual websites can help you locate Irish burials: Find a Grave, BillionGraves, and Interment.net.

Census

Sadly, the pre-1901 censuses were destroyed (with only some fragments surviving). This means that we currently have access only to the 1901 and 1911 censuses and won't have access to any later censuses until the 1926 becomes available in January 2027. The 1901 and 1911 censuses can be accessed at FamilySearch, as well as at the National Archives (Republic of Ireland), Ancestry, and Findmypast.

For more information about Irish research

Books relating to general Irish genealogical research (in addition to the ones mentioned in the previous section on British research) include:

- *Tracing Your Irish Family History on the Internet: A Guide for Family Historians* by Chris Paton, published in 2020
- *Tracing Your Irish Ancestors* (5th ed.) by John Grenham, published in 2019
- *The Family Tree Irish Genealogy Guide: How to Trace Your Ancestors in Ireland* by Claire Santry, published in 2017
- *How to Trace Your Family Tree in England, Ireland, Scotland and Wales* by Kathy Chater, published in 2017
- *Researching Scots-Irish Ancestors: The Essential Genealogical Guide to Early Modern Ulster, 1600-1800* (2nd ed.) by William J. Roulston, published in 2018

Chapter 14:
Generations with Records in Other Languages

There are as many as 7,000 different languages spoken in the world today, although an exact number is impossible to determine as linguists cannot always agree on what constitutes a separate language instead of simply a dialect of some other language. The vast majority of those do not have a written tradition in their cultures, so their genealogical information is usually passed down orally. But when it comes to genealogical record keeping, there are still plenty of different languages to deal with, and that you yourself are likely to encounter as you research your own ancestors back in time, especially the many non-English languages of Europe.

Even within the United States (and its Thirteen Colonies predecessor), you might find that your ancestors attended a church that used Latin in its records. If your ancestors were Jewish, you may find some records written at least partially in Hebrew, such as the engravings on tombstones. You may find that your ancestors were mentioned in non-English newspapers: German, Spanish, Italian, and so forth. And you may be in possession of personal papers, including letters and diaries, that are written in languages other than English.

It's also worth noting that some English-language records may be difficult to work with if they are handwritten or from an earlier time, since handwriting methods have changed in the past few hundred years, and there is lots of vocabulary that is no longer in regular use or that has changed meaning. These early documents are almost as difficult to decipher as a record written in a non-English language.

Before we get into the specifics of different languages, let's talk about some general ideas for how to deal with researching non-English records. If you or a relative can read the language, you'll have fewer problems in this area, but if you can't, you are likely to need help from somewhere.

Unless you are dealing with letters or diaries or newspaper articles, you may need nothing more than knowing how genealogical terms appear in the languages of your ancestors. FamilySearch provides lists of genealogical terms in other languages (for example, the words for birth or marriage or death. To see an index to all of their available word lists in over 30 different languages, go to: familysearch.org/en/wiki/Genealogical_Word_Lists

If you need more help with non-English documents than FamilySearch provides, you may be able to go to Google Translate (translate.google.com) to type in the words to see if they can be translated. There are Facebook groups dedicated to providing translations by volunteers who have expertise in various languages, as well as groups dedicated to different ethnicities who can help. At some point, you may need to hire a professional genealogist with expertise in the language to help with transcribing and translating a record in another language.

Finally, once you have traced your ancestors to parts of the world where the records would have been recorded in languages other than English, make good use of the FamilySearch Wiki. The Wiki has entries for every country, and will point you to the records you need, whether they are on FamilySearch itself, another online repository, or somewhere else.

Latin

You are most likely to find genealogical records written in Latin among Catholic Church records, although a few other Christian denominations used Latin at times. In some cases, the records will be primarily in English but the names will have been written in their Latin form, so that Mary will appear as Maria and William as Gulielmus. Wiktionary has a nice list of Latin names and their English-language equivalents at en.wiktionary.org/wiki/Appendix:Latin_forms_of_English_given_names

German

If you were to survey residents of the United States, and asked them what European ethnicity they have, the largest percentage would refer to German. Many of the earliest American colonists and U.S. settlers were from parts of Europe that are now part of modern Germany, or from nearby German-speaking areas (including Austria and Switzerland). Germany itself didn't unify into a single country until 1871. Prior to that time, your ancestors would have identified as being from such German states as Bavaria, Hanover, Prussia, Saxony, or Wurttemberg (among many others).

Some of the earliest newspapers in the Thirteen Colonies were in German, and more than one thousand eventually were published by the end of the 19th century. However, as later generations learned English and abandoned the use of German, and especially during and after World War I, many German-language newspapers ceased publication, and only a small number continue to be published today. Look for these newspapers in the same databases described in Chapter 8.

If your ancestors attended a German church in the United States, the church records may indicate where in Germany your ancestor was from. Your nearest genealogy library may have a copy of the multi-volume set *German Immigrants in American Church Records*, edited by Roger P. Minert. German church records in the United States and in historical German areas in Europe can be found on FamilySearch.

For more information on doing German genealogical research, I recommend these books by James M. Beidler:

- *The Family Tree German Genealogy Guide: How to Trace Your Germanic Ancestry in Europe*, published in 2014
- *Trace Your German Roots Online: A Complete Guide to German Genealogy Websites*, published in 2016
- *The Family Tree Historical Atlas of Germany*, published in 2019

Also look for books on German genealogy written by Ernest Thode.

Spanish

Large parts of the current United States were once under Spanish control, which means that those areas may have generated a large number of Spanish-language genealogical records. Or your ancestors may be from Mexico or from Spanish-speaking parts of Latin America and the Caribbean (especially Puerto Rico and Cuba). In some cases, you may be able to trace your ancestors back to Spain itself.

Be sure to look for Spanish-language newspapers, some of which continue to be published today.

FamilySearch has been digitizing and indexing many millions of genealogical records from Latin America. Many of these are Catholic church records.

For more information, see George R. Ryskamp's 2009 book *Finding Your Hispanic Roots*, and Lyman D. Platt's 2014 book *Census Records for Latin America and the Hispanic United States*.

Italian

Italian ancestry is still one of the more common ethnicities reported by present-day Americans, and Italians arrived in British America as early as the 1600s. Millions of Italians, especially from the agricultural parts of southern Italy, arrived in the United States beginning in the late 1800s and continuing until World War I.

As with other kinds of European research, the first step in researching your ancestors is to identify their towns of origin. Once you have narrowed the geographic scope of your research, you can use the usual types of records, although not all of these will be online and available for you to see at home. For instance, while a census has been conducted every 10 years, the actual census records may be available only at the archives of the specific Italian province. Look for civil registration records (birth, marriage, and death) and church records on FamilySearch.

Books that will get you started include:

- John Philip Colletta's 2009 book *Finding Your Italian Roots: The Complete Guide for Americans* (2nd ed.)
- Suzanne Russo Adams' 2009 book *Finding Your Italian Ancestors: A Beginner's Guide*
- Melanie Holtz's 2017 book *The Family Tree Italian Genealogy Guide: How to Trace Your Family Tree in Italy*

Polish

As with many other ethnic groups, Polish immigrants were part of some of the earliest history of British America and the United States, but millions of Poles arrived in the 19th century and in the 20th century prior to World War I. Perhaps the thing most confusing to those researching their Polish ancestors is that some of the records may indicate other places of origins, such as Russia, Germany, or Austria-Hungary. This is due to the frequently changing national borders of Poland between the 1700s and World War I. For instance, at the time of U.S. census enumeration, individuals were asked to identify their place of birth but to identify it by the name it had at the time of the census enumeration, not at the time when they were born.

Start by figuring out, if possible, the Polish town your ancestor was from. This will enable you to identify the right location for relevant religious records. Some of these records may be available online at FamilySearch.

To help you along with your Polish research, look for the following books:

- Cecile Wendt Jensen's 2010 book *Sto Lat: A Modern Approach to Polish Genealogy*
- Lisa Alzo's 2016 book *The Family Tree Polish, Czech and Slovak Genealogy Guide: How to Trace Your Family Tree in Eastern Europe*
- Rosemary A. Chorzempa's 2014 book *Polish Roots* (2nd ed.)

French

If you have ancestors from the French-speaking parts of Canada (primarily Quebec, but also in parts of New Brunswick and Ontario as well as other provinces), you are very likely to encounter French-language records. This is also true for some Caribbean islands (Haiti, Guadeloupe, and Martinique, among others) and for parts of South America (French Guiana). And if your ancestors were from the U.S. state of Louisiana, you are likely to encounter some early records in French. Finally, you can find French-language records for ancestors in France, Belgium, and Switzerland.

French-language newspapers existed in the United States at least as early as 1789, and a few continue to be published today. You can locate these in the same way that you located English-language newspapers.

If your ancestors were French-Canadian, be sure to visit Library and Archives Canada (LAC), mentioned in the previous chapter in the Canadian section.

For help with French-Canadian and French research, visit the FamilySearch Research Wiki.

Still other languages

If your ancestors come from a part of the world that hasn't already been mentioned, be sure to visit the FamilySearch Research Wiki. There, you'll be able to see how to start doing research and where the records may be found. Many of these records are on FamilySearch, with countless new records being added every few weeks. Other non-English records can be found on Ancestry and MyHeritage.

Chapter 15: Now What?

This book is a beginner's genealogy how-to book. There is no set length of time that will define you as a beginner. Much will depend on how much time you choose to spend doing genealogical research, what else you choose to read (books, magazine articles, blog posts, social media posts), what podcasts you choose to listen to (I hope you won't mind if I suggest starting with *The Genealogy Guys Podcast*, which I co-host), what videos and tutorials you choose to watch, and what conferences and institutes (face-to-face or virtual) you choose to attend. In other words, the best way to move on from being a beginner is to choose to become a more experienced and educated researcher.

Each beginning genealogist's journey is unique. Except for your own full siblings and your own children and their descendants, you have a set of ancestors that nobody else on the planet has ever had or will have. In this book, we've focused on beginners with ancestors in the United States, but you may have had to jump from some of the earlier chapters directly to the last two chapters if you are descended from recent immigrants. Fortunately, there are countless books, magazine articles, and websites that can get you started on researching your ancestors from wherever in the world they lived. And you can always depend on the FamilySearch Research Wiki to point you in the right direction for every U.S. state and every country.

At some point, you may become frustrated with your research, reaching brick walls that are hard to get around. A good way to remain motivated is to research with others, whether they are close relatives or distant cousins. And then be sure to join one or more genealogy societies, whether they are local, state, or national. By going to their meetings and conferences, you'll meet not only other genealogists that you can share your enthusiasm with, but also those who can help you with your questions and problems and keep you going in the right direction. It might still happen that at some point you decide to set your research aside, and spend time doing other things, but if you do it well, it will still be there for you to come back to when you are ready.

Genealogy is a rewarding and worthwhile hobby (and for many, a profession). It tells stories that are in danger of being lost to time. It keeps our ancestors alive in our memories and in the memories of those we share our research with. It preserves history for future generations.

I hope that you have enjoyed the journey so far, and I hope that you will continue to do so.

Index